Carnegie Commission on Higher Education
Sponsored Research Studies

BREAKING THE ACCESS BARRIERS:
A PROFILE OF TWO-YEAR COLLEGES
Leland L. Medsker and Dale Tillery

ANY PERSON, ANY STUDY:
AN ESSAY ON HIGHER EDUCATION IN THE
UNITED STATES
Eric Ashby

THE NEW DEPRESSION IN HIGHER
EDUCATION:
A STUDY OF FINANCIAL CONDITIONS AT 41
COLLEGES AND UNIVERSITIES
Earl F. Cheit

FINANCING MEDICAL EDUCATION:
AN ANALYSIS OF ALTERNATIVE POLICIES
AND MECHANISMS
Rashi Fein and Gerald I. Weber

HIGHER EDUCATION IN NINE COUNTRIES:
A COMPARATIVE STUDY OF COLLEGES AND
UNIVERSITIES ABROAD
*Barbara B. Burn, Philip G. Altbach, Clark Kerr,
and James A. Perkins*

BRIDGES TO UNDERSTANDING:
INTERNATIONAL PROGRAMS OF AMERICAN
COLLEGES AND UNIVERSITIES
Irwin T. Sanders and Jennifer C. Ward

GRADUATE AND PROFESSIONAL EDUCATION,
1980:
A SURVEY OF INSTITUTIONAL PLANS
Lewis B. Mayhew

THE AMERICAN COLLEGE AND AMERICAN
CULTURE:
SOCIALIZATION AS A FUNCTION OF HIGHER
EDUCATION
Oscar Handlin and Mary F. Handlin

RECENT ALUMNI AND HIGHER EDUCATION:
A SURVEY OF COLLEGE GRADUATES
Joe L. Spaeth and Andrew M. Greeley

CHANGE IN EDUCATIONAL POLICY:
SELF-STUDIES IN SELECTED COLLEGES AND
UNIVERSITIES
Dwight R. Ladd

STATE OFFICIALS AND HIGHER EDUCATION:
A SURVEY OF THE OPINIONS AND
EXPECTATIONS OF POLICY MAKERS IN NINE
STATES
Heinz Eulau and Harold Quinley

ACADEMIC DEGREE STRUCTURES:
INNOVATIVE APPROACHES
PRINCIPLES OF REFORM IN DEGREE
STRUCTURES IN THE UNITED STATES
Stephen H. Spurr

COLLEGES OF THE FORGOTTEN AMERICANS:
A PROFILE OF STATE COLLEGES AND
REGIONAL UNIVERSITIES
E. Alden Dunham

FROM BACKWATER TO MAINSTREAM:
A PROFILE OF CATHOLIC HIGHER
EDUCATION
Andrew M. Greeley

THE ECONOMICS OF THE MAJOR PRIVATE
UNIVERSITIES
William G. Bowen
(Out of print, but available from University Microfilms.)

THE FINANCE OF HIGHER EDUCATION
Howard R. Bowen
(Out of print, but available from University Microfilms.)

ALTERNATIVE METHODS OF FEDERAL
FUNDING FOR HIGHER EDUCATION
Ron Wolk
(Out of print, but available from University Microfilms.)

INVENTORY OF CURRENT RESEARCH ON
HIGHER EDUCATION 1968
Dale M. Heckman and Warren Bryan Martin
(Out of print, but available from University Microfilms.)

*The following technical reports are available from the Carnegie Commission on Higher Education, 1947
Center Street, Berkeley, California 94704.*

RESOURCE USE IN HIGHER EDUCATION:
TRENDS IN OUTPUT AND INPUTS, 1930–1967
June O'Neill

TRENDS AND PROJECTIONS OF PHYSICIANS
IN THE UNITED STATES 1967–2002
Mark S. Blumberg

MAY 1970:
THE CAMPUS AFTERMATH OF CAMBODIA
AND KENT STATE
Richard E. Peterson and John A. Bilorusky

MENTAL ABILITY AND HIGHER EDUCATIONAL
ATTAINMENT IN THE 20TH CENTURY
Paul Taubman and Terrence Wales

AMERICAN COLLEGE AND UNIVERSITY
ENROLLMENT TRENDS IN 1971
Richard E. Peterson

PAPERS ON EFFICIENCY IN THE
MANAGEMENT OF HIGHER EDUCATION
*Alexander M. Mood, Colin Bell,
Lawrence Bogard, Helen Brownlee,
and Joseph McCloskey*

The following reprints are available from the Carnegie Commission on Higher Education, 1947 Center Street, Berkeley, California 94704.

ACCELERATED PROGRAMS OF MEDICAL EDUCATION, *by Mark S. Blumberg, reprinted from* JOURNAL OF MEDICAL EDUCATION, *vol. 46, no. 8, August 1971.**

SCIENTIFIC MANPOWER FOR 1970–1985, *by Allan M. Cartter, reprinted from* SCIENCE, *vol. 172, no. 3979, pp. 132–140, April 9, 1971.*

A NEW METHOD OF MEASURING STATES' HIGHER EDUCATION BURDEN, *by Neil Timm, reprinted from* THE JOURNAL OF HIGHER EDUCATION, *vol. 42, no. 1, pp. 27–33, January 1971.**

REGENT WATCHING, *by Earl F. Cheit, reprinted from* AGB REPORTS, *vol. 13, no. 6, pp. 4–13, March 1971.*

COLLEGE GENERATIONS—FROM THE 1930s TO THE 1960s, *by Seymour M. Lipset and Everett C. Ladd, Jr., reprinted from* THE PUBLIC INTEREST, *no. 25, Summer 1971.*

AMERICAN SOCIAL SCIENTISTS AND THE GROWTH OF CAMPUS POLITICAL ACTIVISM IN THE 1960s, *by Everett C. Ladd, Jr., and Seymour M. Lipset, reprinted from* SOCIAL SCIENCES INFORMATION, *vol. 10, no. 2, April 1971.*

THE POLITICS OF AMERICAN POLITICAL SCIENTISTS, *by Everett C. Ladd, Jr., and Seymour M. Lipset, reprinted from* PS, *vol. 4, no. 2, Spring 1971.**

THE DIVIDED PROFESSORIATE, *by Seymour M. Lipset and Everett C. Ladd, Jr., reprinted from* CHANGE, *vol. 3, no. 3, pp. 54–60, May 1971.**

JEWISH ACADEMICS IN THE UNITED STATES: THEIR ACHIEVEMENTS, CULTURE AND POLITICS, *by Seymour M. Lipset and Everett C. Ladd, Jr., reprinted from* AMERICAN JEWISH YEAR BOOK, *1971.*

THE UNHOLY ALLIANCE AGAINST THE CAMPUS, *by Kenneth Keniston and Michael Lerner, reprinted from* NEW YORK TIMES MAGAZINE, *November 8, 1970 .*

PRECARIOUS PROFESSORS: NEW PATTERNS OF REPRESENTATION, *by Joseph W. Garbarino, reprinted from* INDUSTRIAL RELATIONS, *vol. 10, no. 1, February 1971.**

. . . AND WHAT PROFESSORS THINK: ABOUT STUDENT PROTEST AND MANNERS, MORALS, POLITICS, AND CHAOS ON THE CAMPUS, *by Seymour Martin Lipset and Everett Carll Ladd, Jr., reprinted from* PSYCHOLOGY TODAY, *November 1970.**

DEMAND AND SUPPLY IN U.S. HIGHER EDUCATION: A PROGRESS REPORT, *by Roy Radner and Leonard S. Miller, reprinted from* AMERICAN ECONOMIC REVIEW, *May 1970.**

RESOURCES FOR HIGHER EDUCATION: AN ECONOMIST'S VIEW, by Theodore W. Schultz, reprinted from JOURNAL OF POLITICAL ECONOMY, vol. 76, no. 3, University of Chicago, May/June 1968.*

INDUSTRIAL RELATIONS AND UNIVERSITY RELATIONS, by Clark Kerr, reprinted from PROCEEDINGS OF THE 21ST ANNUAL WINTER MEETING OF THE INDUSTRIAL RELATIONS RESEARCH ASSOCIATION, pp. 15–25.*

NEW CHALLENGES TO THE COLLEGE AND UNIVERSITY, by Clark Kerr, reprinted from Kermit Gordon (ed.), AGENDA FOR THE NATION, The Brookings Institution, Washington, D.C., 1968.*

PRESIDENTIAL DISCONTENT, by Clark Kerr, reprinted from David C. Nichols (ed.), PERSPECTIVES ON CAMPUS TENSIONS: PAPERS PREPARED FOR THE SPECIAL COMMITTEE ON CAMPUS TENSIONS, American Council on Education, Washington, D.C., September 1970.*

STUDENT PROTEST—AN INSTITUTIONAL AND NATIONAL PROFILE, by Harold Hodgkinson, reprinted from THE RECORD, vol. 71, no. 4, May 1970.*

WHAT'S BUGGING THE STUDENTS?, by Kenneth Keniston, reprinted from EDUCATIONAL RECORD, American Council on Education, Washington, D.C., Spring 1970.*

THE POLITICS OF ACADEMIA, by Seymour Martin Lipset, reprinted from David C. Nichols (ed.), PERSPECTIVES ON CAMPUS TENSIONS: PAPERS PREPARED FOR THE SPECIAL COMMITTEE ON CAMPUS TENSIONS, American Council on Education, Washington, D.C., September 1970.*

INTERNATIONAL PROGRAMS OF U.S. COLLEGES AND UNIVERSITIES: PRIORITIES FOR THE SEVENTIES, by James A. Perkins, reprinted by permission of the International Council for Educational Development, Occasional Paper no. 1, July 1971.

FACULTY UNIONISM: FROM THEORY TO PRACTICE, by Joseph W. Garbarino, reprinted from INDUSTRIAL RELATIONS, vol. 11, no. 1, pp. 1–17, February 1972.

MORE FOR LESS: HIGHER EDUCATION'S NEW PRIORITY, by Virginia B. Smith, reprinted from UNIVERSAL HIGHER EDUCATION: COSTS AND BENEFITS, American Council on Education, Washington, D.C., 1971.

ACADEMIA AND POLITICS IN AMERICA, by Seymour M. Lipset, reprinted from Thomas J. Nossiter (ed.), IMAGINATION AND PRECISION IN THE SOCIAL SCIENCES, pp. 211–289, Faber and Faber, London, 1972.

POLITICS OF ACADEMIC NATURAL SCIENTISTS AND ENGINEERS, by Everett C. Ladd, Jr., and Seymour M. Lipset, reprinted from SCIENCE, vol. 176, no. 4039, pp. 1091–1100, June 9, 1972.

THE INTELLECTUAL AS CRITIC AND REBEL: WITH SPECIAL REFERENCE TO THE UNITED STATES AND THE SOVIET UNION, by Seymour M. Lipset and Richard B. Dobson, reprinted from DAEDALUS, vol. 101, no. 3, pp. 137–198, Summer 1972.

THE NATURE AND ORIGINS OF THE CARNEGIE COMMISSION ON HIGHER EDUCATION, *by Alan Pifer, reprinted by permission of The Carnegie Foundation for the Advancement of Teaching, speech delivered Oct. 16, 1972.*

THE DISTRIBUTION OF ACADEMIC TENURE IN AMERICAN HIGHER EDUCATION, *by Martin Trow, reprinted from* THE TENURE DEBATE, *Bardwell Smith (ed.), Jossey-Bass, San Francisco, 1972.*

THE POLITICS OF AMERICAN SOCIOLOGISTS, *by Seymour M. Lipset and Everett C. Ladd, Jr., reprinted from* THE AMERICAN JOURNAL OF SOCIOLOGY, *vol. 78, no. 1, July 1972.*

*The Commission's stock of this reprint has been exhausted.

In reviewing this history, marked by the actions of great university presidents, Professor Storr establishes a background for coming to grips with the confusion about the meaning of degrees that colors so much of graduate education today. To clear up this confusion, to bring substance and form into closer correspondence, graduate study within the university must acquire new meaning. What should that meaning be? Upon the answer hangs the resolution of the self-defeating and oversimplified confrontations that pit college against graduate school, human relevance against professionalism, and teaching against research.

Drawing upon history, Storr in his concluding chapter explores two approaches to such a resolution. Basic to both is the belief that inquiry and research must be clearly distinguished. Then the graduate school must choose explicitly what each degree represents. As this profile makes clear, the choices made now will have a critical effect on the future of graduate education.

Richard J. Storr is professor of history and humanities at York University in Toronto. Last year he served as acting dean of the Faculty of Graduate Studies at York.

This profile is the fourteenth in a series prepared for the Carnegie Commission on Higher Education.

The Beginning of the Future

McGraw-Hill Book Company
Serving Man's Need for Knowledge
1221 Avenue of the Americas
New York, New York 10020

The Beginning
of the Future

A HISTORICAL APPROACH TO GRADUATE EDUCATION

IN THE ARTS AND SCIENCES

by *Richard J. Storr*

Professor of History and Humanities
York University, Toronto

Fourteenth of a Series of Profiles Sponsored by
The Carnegie Commission on Higher Education

MC GRAW-HILL BOOK COMPANY
New York   St. Louis   San Francisco   Düsseldorf
London   Sydney   Toronto   Mexico   Panama
Johannesburg   Kuala Lumpur   Montreal
New Delhi   Rio de Janeiro   Singapore

THE BEGINNING OF THE FUTURE
A Historical Approach to Graduate Education in the Arts and Sciences

Library of Congress Cataloging in Publication Data

Storr, Richard J
The beginning of the future. . . .
"Fourteenth of a series of profiles sponsored by the
Carnegie Commission on Higher Education."
Bibliography: p.
1. Universities and colleges—United States—
Graduate work—History. 2. Degrees, Academic—
United States. I. Carnegie Commission on Higher
Education. II. Title.
LA228.5.S74   378.1'553'0973   72-10539
ISBN 0-07-010056-X

123456789MAMM79876543

For Jinny

Contents

Foreword

Throughout the short history of graduate education in the United States, there has been a strong connection between innovation and vitality. Today, because of the expansion of knowledge, the growth of interdisciplinary fields, the shrinking job market for postgraduate degree holders, and the blurred meaning of graduate degrees, there is a critical need to give wise direction to whatever innovation is undertaken. What is done at this juncture in history will influence the future of higher education for years to come.

In this thoughtful and incisive profile, Richard Storr reviews the past in order to get some guideposts for the future. A sharper, more subtle understanding of the options academics faced in the past, he says, can liberate our thinking about the choices we must make for the future. Basic to this understanding is a sure grasp of the relationship between substance and form. For example, Storr asks, "Why does the potentially creative tension between . . . the impulse to do research and Ph.D. requirements, sometimes degenerate into wasteful conflict in which imagination struggles to free itself from formalism, mechanical standards, bureaucracy, and the lot? On the other side: where should the dismantling of forms stop lest the mind simply be left floundering?"

During the half-century that preceded Yale's awarding of the first Ph.D. degree in 1861, several unsuccessful attempts were made to establish a national university with uniform standards. Yale's action put an end to any more such attempts and by the end of the nineteenth century, spurred on by the example of the Johns Hopkins University, graduate education in the United States had become a theme with many variations. The theme was that Ph.D. study and research went together, underlaid by faith in the unity of inquiry. With the research went the methods of science, which at the time was experiencing rapid expansion. In the twentieth century, however, this relationship between research and the Ph.D. underwent several shifts, until today the word *research* as applied to Ph.D. work is in some disarray.

To clarify matters, Storr recommends that *research* and *inquiry* be thought of separately and be given distinct meanings. If this is done, and if the graduate schools determine explicitly what each degree represents, graduate education will have taken a major step toward determining its own character.

In an earlier Carnegie Commission book, *Academic Degree Structures: Innovative Approaches,* Stephen Spurr reviewed the history of graduate degrees in America and Western Europe and then offered his own "idealized and generalized" degree structure for American higher education. Professor Storr, in the concluding chapter of this essay, suggests two patterns for a new degree structure, both of which attempt to resolve such controversies as those that pit college against graduate school, human relevance against professionalism, and teaching against research. Both also parallel recommendations made in the Commission reports *Less Time, More Options* and *The More Effective Use of Resources* in that they aim to bring degrees and degree requirements into the closest possible correspondence with the potentiality of higher study and the need of society that it flourish. Professor Storr has himself given us a valuable guidepost to the future of higher education.

Clark Kerr
Chairman
The Carnegie Commission
on Higher Education

January 1973

Acknowledgments

What is often said at the beginning of books is painfully true of this essay. It draws both upon a welling pool of scholarship and upon the thought of many friends: it is impossible to thank by name everyone who has helped me. It is part of the argument here that one cannot think to best advantage about graduate education without taking account of the writing on the history of American higher education: certainly this essay could not have been written if the historical literature were not as rich as it is. Especially but not exclusively in regard to collegiate education, the list of books to which the footnotes refer by no means exhausts the sources from which the generalizations presented here were distilled. I must speak particularly, however, of the late Professor Arthur M. Schlesinger, Sr., who encouraged and directed my first effort to understand graduate education historically, and of Professor Paul Buck, who clarified an idea which runs through this book. I must speak also of numberless conversations about graduate education with colleagues at the University of Chicago. I am similarly indebted to my colleagues at York University, especially to the members of the Graduate History Programme and to Dean Michael Collie and the members of two committees that have designed an interdisciplinary master's program at York. I am very grateful to Margaret Bowman, Katharine Bush, Anne Iannetta, Audrey Robinson, Stanley Vittoz, and John Wadland for their assistance. I have drawn heavily upon an earlier book of mine, *The Beginnings of Graduate Education in America* (copyright 1953 by the University of Chicago), with the consent of the publisher; the Macmillan Company has renewed permission for me to use two passages appearing in *The Diary of George Templeton Strong,* edited by Allan Nevins and Milton H. Thomas (copyright 1952 by The Macmillan Company, New York). I also thank the Harvard University Archives for materials copied some 30 years ago from the Benjamin Peirce papers but not used until now. Two members of the staff of the Carnegie Commission, Verne A. Stadtman and Sidney J. P. Hollister, have my thanks, too, for their help as this manuscript was being written and prepared for the press.

The Beginning of the Future

1. The Uses of History

It could be said that this essay was begun in 1937 at the massive, well-rubbed seminar table of the department of history at the Johns Hopkins University. A half-century earlier a group of students, many of whom were to become distinguished academics—and one a President of the United States—had gathered around that same table to discuss history and the social sciences under the eye of one of the great entrepreneurs of American scholarship, Herbert Baxter Adams. Woodrow Wilson did not have the experience in that seminar that was to move Josiah Royce, a sometime student in another department of the university, to draw upon poetry when he recalled his youth: The beginning of the university had been a dawn in which 'twas bliss to be alive. Opinions about the university had differed, but, when I was a first-year graduate student there in 1937–38, one could not help but sense that something remarkable had happened at the Johns Hopkins in the years just after its opening in 1876. While the university was demonstrating to the nation, as one understood, that graduate study was a viable sequel to college education, the students had discovered that the pursuit of scholarship was intellectually fructifying. The Hopkins was such a place for me, too, but with a difference. Professor Stull Holt was introducing the demographic study that was to flourish in historical scholarship some 20 years later; but I missed that cue. Taking graduate courses, however valuable professionally, seemed a let-down intellectually and not an acceleration of the thinking that I had come to expect as an undergraduate. College had meant Swarthmore in a period of the Aydelotte era when the honors seminars, although no longer experimental, were producing great intellectual excitement. The mid-thirties was a time when honors work had passed its dawning, but it was a fresh morning in which it was indeed bliss to be thinking. Inquiry became superlatively

1

important, so one came away from college with a hunger for far-ranging inquiry that graduate study in general did not satisfy and research-training in particular appeared to frustrate. Had graduate education, then, changed drastically in substance since 1876? Thanks to a Hopkins tradition of what now seems an arcadian freedom from bureaucracy, it was possible to look for answers to that question, quite apart from formal course work—which meant, as one realized later, that the substance of graduate study at the Hopkins had not in fact altogether changed. I began to read through the early records of the history seminar and of the university itself to discover what had happened in the beginning. The more I read, however, the clearer it became that, although Johns Hopkins had been immensely vital, its opening had not been the beginning of graduate education in the United States.

While I was pursuing the origins of that education, and later while I examined phases of its history that followed the opening of the Johns Hopkins, I was confronted repeatedly by the fact of academic innovation. (I had encountered it already as a student at Swarthmore as well as at home during Joseph Brewer's administration of Olivet College; and I was to encounter it again while a faculty member at the University of Chicago and at York University.) Plainly a connection existed between innovation and intellectual vitality. It could not be assumed that every new departure would foster inquiry, but some certainly did. The questions multiplied, starting with the puzzle that is perhaps the easiest to put and the hardest to solve: What is the relation of substance to form in graduate education? How are fresh aspirations embodied in new institutions in such manner that intellectual energy is released? Why does the potentially creative tension between substance and form, say between the impulse to do research and Ph.D. requirements, sometimes degenerate into wasteful conflict in which imagination struggles to free itself from formalism, mechanical standards, bureaucracy, and the lot? On the other side: Where should the dismantling of forms stop lest the mind simply be left floundering?

History cannot give direct answers to questions of that kind, but I submit both that they must be faced during any planning for the future and that they will be answered with the greatest wisdom where there is understanding of the innovations that produced graduate education in the past. Such understanding has particular point in the American setting.

The traditions of many American universities stem from a time when each was a new university, not only in the sense that it had just been opened but also in the sense that it staked its reputation—or its hopes for reputation—upon success in accomplishing something novel. A tradition of innovation exists, and pride in one's university is for many Americans associated not only with superlative achievements in scholarship and science but also with the imagination and determination one's university possessed to try institutionally what had not been done before. Yale is often called conservative, but it granted the first Ph.D. degrees and is proud of the fact. The leaflets of fund-raising campaigns give ample evidence that among universities a record of pioneering is deemed a financial asset, but pride in past innovation goes far deeper than the exploitation of history for material gain. Such pride is inextricably connected with a concept of greatness in a university. If Americans talk more often of great universities than other peoples, they may do so because Americans have acquired a characteristic admiration for academic enterprise and see in the attempt to innovate something that can only be called great. Perhaps no university president has acquired fame as a leader of political radicalism, but how many are happily remembered for their academic conservatism? A brilliant period in the history of a university is frequently equated with a presidential administration: Tappan's Michigan, White's Cornell, Eliot's Harvard, Gilman's Hopkins. The list goes on, and its length helps to explain why the idea of innovation has been driven deep into the minds of Americans. We believe in heroes, and it is important to examine what is thought of as the heroic age of graduate education—the more so because some of its forms are still in use. (If an archaeologist a thousand years hence unearths only the bare doctoral requirements from about 1910 on to tell him what twentieth-century culture was, he may conclude that the "Ph.D. people" stagnated.)

But nostalgia can be dynamic. It has been remarked that the backward look can inspire rather than obstruct reform. Behind the Declaration of Independence, there was the conviction that George III had sinned against a traditional British liberty. The Jacksonian Democrats revamped American political life partly in the name of an Old Republic. In the field of education, the manifesto of progressivism, John Dewey's *The School and Society,* was published with a picture of a child at a spinning wheel on the cover. Would some programs for academic revolution take quite the form that they do if memory, or a myth, of the small college in its heyday did not inspire belief that intimacy and fellowship are possible in the academy? Nevertheless, admiration for the innovators of the past imposes an obligation. The task is not archaelogical. There is no use restoring what they built as an academic Williamsburg; rather, the task is to understand what innovation entails. It is not enough to coast, however fast, like a spaceship moving on the momentum of an explosion in the past. What is required is to know what made that explosion possible. At the least, innovation calls not only for the inventiveness that enables somebody to supply devices that everybody feels the need of, but also for the capacity to see the possibilities of situations that nobody else has noticed. And innovation requires at bottom an exercise of will as well as the discovery of ideas. The past reforms we call great would have meant little or nothing if the reformers had not given their programs a thrust derived from conviction and a readiness to accept the risks of trying the untried.

In 1767, Ezra Stiles, an intellectual ancestor of the nineteenth-century academic reformers, argued that factual narration reaches perfection only when "the motives and *Springs of Action* are fairly laid open and arise into view with all their Effects about them. . . ." Indeed, to understand what graduate education as an innovation was—and what it is as well—it is necessary to search out its springs of action (Morgan, 1962, p. 146).

But first a word about the use of history in the framing of academic policy and about the way that use is affected by the first person singular: As a topic of historical writing, academic life resembles an inkblot, and a book about an academic institution may reveal as much, indirectly, about the author's own hopes or fears for higher education in the future as it tells, directly, about the nature of the institution in the past. It may be true, too—indeed it may be unavoidably so—that a book about higher education will imply the history of the author's academic experience no less than it presents a history of the topic in hand. Such a book should be recognized as being a cousin, however detached in mood, of the personal essay—and I submit that the same is true of proposals for the future. It is an irony of education that nobody can write about it without giving evidence on an issue that is of central importance to graduate education: Is objective knowledge possible? Yet does it follow that, because we each stand somewhere in particular, we can safely read whatever we please into—or out of—history? Examination of the past can be made to yield something other than the shallowest impressionism or the grossest kind of subjective opinion to the degree that we recognize precisely where it is that descriptive statements of fact and normative judgments fuse. Where we mistake the judgment for the fact, we may too easily persuade ourselves that history is on our side; and when we work from a past that never was, we may create a future that we never wanted. True, no great harm is done if we fail to challenge those historical references that are patently used (and can be readily dismissed) as rhetorical ornament. We may deceive ourselves tragically, however, when we draw upon history uncritically as a source of authority and a key to reality. It is no more important to admit that we can be only more or less right about the past than to understand that we can be more or less wrong, too—and that the more wrong we are, the greater is the cost of self-deception.

During a period of some 40 years, critical inquiry into general academic movements as well as particular universities has been underway in the circle of professional historians. (Scholars in other disciplines have also been at work on much the same topics.) The historical development of American higher education and of American life as it has been exhibited in and influenced by the academy has become the target of the same close scrutiny that historians have directed at politics, diplomacy, and the economy: it is relevant to the theme of this essay that graduate students in history have truly contributed to knowledge while writing Ph.D. theses on aspects of higher education. What has been happening historiographically is that, as the universities have been gaining ever wider recognition as fundamental institutions, the historians have been treating American higher education ever more fully as a topic of the most serious scholarship. The result of their study has not been the appearance of *the* history of American higher education but rather, the ventilation of academic tradition. Where we once may have thought we saw unity in purpose and simplicity in means, we can now detect ambiguity and complexity. Of much that once appeared inevitable, we must say that it remains to be proved that it had to happen that way; and where we still sense a kind of inevitability— say, that the immense growth of American capital and technology was bound to have an effect on higher education—we find that pat statements of cause and effect leave much out. Where we see creative minds at work in the past, we have a clearer view of their situations and resources and thus of what it was that they created. It is possible to have a sharper, more subtle understanding of the options academics faced in the past, and such awareness has a liberating impact on the way in which we think about our choices for the future.

History *is* invoked frequently — not only by professional historians — and perhaps more often than we have stopped to notice. In just one recent collection of papers on "The Embattled University" (*Daedalus,* Winter 1970), these historical statements appear, one being by a historian but the others coming from authors who are identified professionally with sociology, education (as an academic discipline), biology, psychology, philosophy, industrial relations, and academic administration:

For a very long time it has been believed in this country that talented youth of humble origins should go to college.

Historically, educational institutions have performed functions in American society which have not always been perceived and which are only related to intellectual goals by a combination of peculiarly American factors.

Traditionally, our universities have had three functions — education, scholarship, and service.

Diplomas and degrees were originally invented to make stages in a carefully planned educational sequence and were awarded not only for having reached the appropriate chronological point without academic mishap, but for having met some definite and definitely situated challenge, such as a series of examinations.

The American system [of academic governance] bears the marks of its origins in the Protestant sects of the early colonies.

Historically, the university has had as one of its functions the integrative role of nurturing the values of society and transmitting them to succeeding generations.

Yesterday's university could not really be accused of sanctifying the feudal or the capitalist order.

And then these clashing statements:

The central function of higher education in America has always been vocational.

The liberal arts college has traditionally been a place where the student is taught not how to do a certain job, but how to attack and think about certain problems.[1]

[1] "The Embattled University," *Daedalus,* Winter 1970: Martin Trow, p. 3; Jill Conway, pp. 43–44; S. E. and Zella Luria, p. 76; Peter J. Caws, p. 95; Clark Kerr, p. 110; Ralph A. Dungan, p. 143; Stanley Hoffman, p. 191; Edgar Z. Friedenberg, p. 56; Morris B. Abram, p. 126.

None of these statements is an antiquarian tidbit. Each touches on a highly charged issue—social mobility, the uniqueness of American education, the functions of higher education, the relation of the American university to society, etc.—and in regard to these matters we must make choices. As we do, are we to be satisfied with the idea that, as a guidepost, any view of the past will serve as well as another? Are we content to shrug off the contradiction between the last two statements? It makes a difference whether we act according to the proposition that American higher education has become what it is because there have been jobs to fill. What weight *have* Americans given to vocationalism or, to speak particularly of graduate education, professionalism?

The use of history is not confined to the thought of individual academics; history has been given a place in the making of formal policy. Reports often open with a historical survey accompanied by charts indicating growth or decline in enrollment, costs, or whatever the topic in hand is. The logic of a whole report may be influenced by implicitly historical judgments where a comparison between purposes or practice in the past and the present situation is the hinge upon which a program for future action swings. Consider a common pattern of argument: Your committee finds that the institution has been moving in a particular direction; we are satisfied—or dissatisfied—with the place at which we have arrived; therefore we recommend no—or so much—change in our course. A now classic argument at once exemplifies the pattern and raises a substantive question that lies near the heart of much controversy over graduate education. It has been asserted time and again that Ph.D. studies were instituted and have been pursued as training in research, that the impact of such training upon undergraduate instruction is intolerable, and that a new kind of doctorate for college professors must be devised. Is it important whether that argument is historically sound? Our first, quick answer may be that every professor, if not yet every schoolboy, knows that the Ph.D. has always been a research degree. But is that answer sufficient where the stakes are high? Thanks to critical scholarship, historical writing is full of the exploded bits of facts that everybody once took for granted. Close scrutiny of historical judgments may show that common understanding, even presented in bald propositions, may not be far from the mark; but it may also show that a simple yes-or-no verdict obscures nuances of meaning that ought not to be overlooked. A research degree may have one effect if research means highly compartmentalized fact-finding as an end in itself and a very different effect if research stands for disciplined pursuit of new ideas, as distinct from the elaboration of dogma. What, then, has research meant?

Although antihistorical currents are moving in the university, history-mindedness has tinctured academic culture deeply. In most nonacademic institutions, historical study is established, if at all, as an auxiliary service, but at the university, it has a major claim on the budget. By far the larger part of the historical profession is composed of professors of history. Departments of history, however, hold no patent upon the historical approach. The partitions between historical studies, so designated, and much inquiry in archaeology, anthropology, sociology, literature, economics, political science, geography, etc., are paper-thin and full of holes; indeed the argument was made at the University of Chicago some years ago that so much history was studied outside of the department of history itself that it had ceased to have a claim upon a distinct territory of its own. The presumption is that historians, with or without portfolio, are changing hats and not habits of mind when they move from scholarly pursuits to academic affairs: it may well be that a disproportionately large number of historians become deans and presidents. The a priori case must be that the impact of the historical approach is great.

It does not follow, however, that a professional, explicitly analytical reference to history exhausts the possibilities of its use. The least observation of committees in session indicates that there is at work something that might be called *curriculum vitae* history were it not that such documents leave out that part of autobiography that may be most significant during debate. I refer to the impulse to measure proposals for change against what has touched one's own life in the university and to the pooling of memories that occurs during the process of arriving at or maintaining standards. Is there any doubt but that they reflect not only more or less abstract principle, and perhaps vested interests, but also remembered experience, either happy or bitter? It would certainly appear that much of the passion that discussion of standards arouses is the fruit of anxiety lest the worth of what one has known and admired should be jeopardized. How often have allegedly impersonal and inhumane regulations been maintained really because they express a personal and intensely human, if not always humane, fidelity to great teaching or great teachers recalled to mind as templates of excellence? Explicit reminiscence need not be the vehicle of comparison between memory and proposed change; it is enough that there occurs such a matching up in the back of the mind as gives rise either to fear or to hope that history will not repeat itself. The mythology of a university can serve as an extension of personal memory and may similarly be used as a test of policy: it may be said of a proposed program either that we have never done *that* here or that maybe we should give it a try because we have always welcomed experimentation. Both responses take their force from something very like folk history, and either may decide the issue before other, more critical, thought is put under way. Such informal, as it were, intuitive history may not be deliberately chosen in place of the more analytical kind because it may not be seen that there is a choice to make at all. Informal history is often highly charged emotionally, and it may simply expand to preempt any intellectual space the other might have occupied.

Patently, the danger is that the uses of personal history will be blindly reactionary, in the ordinary as well as in the root sense of the word. Such history can produce both a bullheaded refusal to recognize that the status quo has faults and a compulsive radicalism springing from rejection of a past bitterly remembered. The Right and the Left can abuse history in the same stupid way, but this by no means proves that consulting personal history is intrinsically bad practice. It would be a disaster—and the university would indeed be a lifeless place—if debate over policy never had its start in personal reactions, either to the fact of a threat to something held dear or to the presence of some injustice and folly too long ignored. Abuse occurs not because such history *is* personal but because the same closeness to deeply felt experience that makes personal history irreplaceable may prevent the people employing it from seeing how partial it is. The remedy is not to outlaw remembered experience but to put it into a more spacious and less private setting. The first person singular is the starting point, but the level of consciousness in the university will be determined by the distance beyond autobiography that every academic climbs.

2. In the Age of the College

"We begin our work . . . after costly ventures of which we reap the lessons, while others bear the loss" (Storr, 1953, p. 134). That retrospective thought was in Daniel Coit Gilman's mind while he was being inaugurated as first president of the Johns Hopkins University in 1876. The ventures of the past had yielded a variety of models for the organization of graduate education. They had also given expression to an ideal. The pressure of that ideal explains much of what Gilman was attempting and much of the impact that his accomplishment was to have. When had the lessons begun? It would be straining for remote origins to find the beginning of American graduate education in a seventeenth-century gift that Lady Anne Radcliffe Mowlson made to Harvard for the support of M.A. candidates. The donation is a reminder that the American college was not always supposed to be concerned exclusively with undergraduates; however, Lady Mowlson's particular intention was neglected. In the next century Yale kept distinct accounts for a bequest made by Bishop George Berkeley for support of three "scholars of the house" or holders of bachelor's degrees who showed proficiency in Latin and Greek. It may be that an earned M.A. was not wholly lost to sight even when it became customary to grant the M.A. degree in course, i.e., without requirement of formal study. It is possible to detect the germ of graduate studies in Ezra Stiles' planning and policy as president of Yale after 1777. He saw a distinction not only between a grammar school and a college but also between a college and a university; and he advocated the establishment of professorships in several fields of the arts and sciences as well as of law and medicine. Stiles also insisted that the best scholars should be appointed the tutors of undergraduates. As a tutor was usually appointed just after graduating and was eligible to become scholar of the house before taking an M.A., the Yale system of faculty recruitment in Stiles' time worked to produce a scholarly group not unlike a body of teaching assistants with some fellowship support. Thus some ideas and devices resembling pieces of graduate education had been defined at Yale, but they were neither thought of as parts of the pattern we know nor given the chance, as the establishment of professorships aborted, to develop into another kind of graduate education (Morison, 1935, pp. 307–312; Morgan, 1962, p. 399).

While Stiles was at work in New Haven, Thomas Jefferson proposed a reorganization of the College of William and Mary that also involved a distinction between college and university, but again the elevation of a college to the level of university instruction was impracticable. Because neither Yale nor William and Mary had money to support successful reform, both efforts seem shadowy, but they were not parochial. Both were related to the movements that were reshaping American life. It was neither an accident nor an aberration that Jefferson and Stiles, both patriots, turned to academic reform in the midst of the Revolution. It was as a citizen of the independent state of Virginia, which was bent upon revising the whole body of its laws in the light of its new liberty, that Jefferson concerned himself with William and Mary: Jefferson's plan for its reorganization was one among many recommendations for the structural reform of Virginia society. Similarly, Stiles was moved by the pride and patriotism of the Revolution and its aftermath to plan institutions grander and more elevated than the existing colleges. They had, Stiles said (Morgan, 1962, p. 323), spread the seeds of knowledge that made possible the conduct of American affairs "with that Wisdom, Magnanimity, and Glory, which already astonishes Europe and will honor us to the whole World and to the latest Posterity"; but the process of education was not complete. (See also Malone, 1948, pp. 284–285.)

The same sense of unfinished business that moved Stiles in 1777 was in the mind of another patriot, Dr. Benjamin Rush, a decade later—in the year when the Constitution was drafted in his own city—when he declared: "THE REVOLUTION IS NOT OVER." To complete it, Rush thought, the Congress must not only restore the public credit, provide for defense, and revive commerce; it should also appropriate money for a national university. The inspiration of the citizenry with federal ideals (which meant republicanism) could only be effected "by our young men meeting and spending two or three years together in a national university, and afterwards disseminating their knowledge and principles through every county, township, and village of the united states [sic]" (Storr, 1953, p. 7). Presumably Rush was thinking of the same distinction between college and university that he had observed a year earlier when planning an educational system for Pennsylvania. In 1789, John Fenno, later to become a Federalist spokesman, also saw a need for such institutions as a federal university to remove local views and habits: college graduates would attend the university for two or three years of additional study. Similar proposals appeared in projects prepared by Samuel Knox, president of Frederick Academy in Maryland, and Samuel Harrison Smith, a Jeffersonian editor, who were the two winners of a prize offered by the American Philosophical Society for essays on liberal education adapted to the American genius of government. Neither Knox nor Smith set a limit to the university work following upon that of the college; indeed, Knox proposed that a student should be allowed to stay as long as he pleased at the university, on a salary "in consideration of his devoting his time to the cultivation of science or literature, in which last case, he shall become a fellow of the University" (Storr, 1953, pp. 7–8). In 1806 Samuel Harrison Smith published a similar proposal by Joel Barlow, who was a member of the American Philosophical Society and—perhaps not quite incidentally—had graduated from Yale during Stiles' administration. Barlow envisaged a national institution that would serve both as a university (or a set of universities) and as a national academy to foster research (Madsen, 1966, pp. 38–42, 46–50).

The recognized need for institutions to promote national unity helps to explain why political leaders of the country became interested in a national university. In 1796, President George Washington thought it of the highest importance that the young men of the country should assemble together in the period of life when friendships are formed and habits established. They would discover "that there was not that cause for those jealousies and prejudices which one part of the union had imbibed against another part" (Madsen, 1966, p. 30). Washington also supported a national university because he believed that education abroad eroded the republican principles of American students. Congress was loathe to pay for a university, but Washington attempted personally to provide support for it by writing a donation of stock into his will. While serving as President, Jefferson was familiar with Barlow's project of 1806 and in fact made corrections in a draft of it. In the same year, Jefferson officially recommended that public lands be set aside as an endowment. He had increasingly serious doubts about the constitutionality of a national university, however, and because of the same doubts, his successor, James Madison, failed to move very aggressively. Yet as a member of the Constitutional Convention, he had long since proposed an article on a national university; and as President he did recommend establishment of a national seminary of learning in the District of Columbia. Sale of vacant lands there would support the university: plainly Madison was trying to make the most use he could of congressional authority in the District. Again, a seminary would foster and disseminate "national feelings." President James Monroe also appreciated the force of the constitutional question and suggested that a constitutional amendment in regard to internal improvements should include a provision giving Congress power to institute seminaries of learning. It was in the context of internal improvements, too, that President John Quincy Adams called attention to the fact that Washington's hopes for a national university had not been fulfilled. As the nation approached the fiftieth anniversary of independence, the nuances of thought about a national university were changing. A utilitarianism that Rush had expressed was on the rise, while the vision of a national university as a central tabernacle of republicanism was growing dim (Madsen, 1966, pp. 43–56).

Although the idea of a national university has never died, the repeated failure of efforts to float such an institution has perhaps left the impression that the project was inherently chimerical, or just pretentiously wrongheaded, from the beginning. Yet the idea helps — partly by providing a contrast — to put the later development of graduate education into perspective. The projects for a national university gave some currency to the idea — often in high places and among circles of very able men — that American higher education should serve a political purpose. Although one can detect characteristically Jeffersonian overtones in the worry over constitutionality, as well as some federalism, in Washington's attitude, the founding of a national university was not a party issue. Doubtless some of the writing was designed to foreshadow, or presupposed the existence of, a governing elite, but the national university was often presented as the crown of an educational system for the whole people. Doubtless, too, popular education implied what now would be recognized as indoctrination, but the principle to be taught, republicanism, was conceived of as being new, fragile, and desperately exposed to attack. In the writing, anxiety provided the counterpoint to pride in the new political dispensation. So long as republicanism was in jeopardy, an American could believe that defense of the principle that gave the national interest its essential character required not merely higher education but the highest education conceivable. The perilous state of the Union inspired some Americans to devise a university that had no ceiling whatsoever. The genius of American government—in the phrase of the American Philosophical Society—put its own premium upon the play of imagination.

The ordering of education by levels figures largely in the projects for a national university. Their authors were rationalizers of education, accustomed to constitution framing as a mode of thought. The conscious articulation of jurisdictions and electorates, often in layers, was familiar work; the formal organization of education in the states, perhaps with a "university" at the top, was second nature. But blueprints had to be revised, and the universities that they called for did not become graduate schools. It is a commonplace of history that Thomas Jefferson turned to the foundation of a state university after his retirement from active politics. The plan out of which the University of Virginia emerged had much in common with the national university projects except that from the Jeffersonian point of view a program for a state system of education had the advantage of not raising a constitutional question. The original bill that Joseph C. Cabell, Jefferson's lieutenant, presented to the House of Delegates called for a structure with three stories—an idea that Jefferson had long held. The young Virginian would go first to a ward school, then to a college, and finally to the university where all branches of useful knowledge would be taught. The Board of Commissioners who planned the university did argue that the nature of knowledge demanded something more than existing colleges: "Each generation . . . must advance the knowledge and well-being of mankind, not *infinitely,* as some have said, but *indefinitely,* and to a term which no one can fix and foresee" (Storr, 1953, pp. 12–13). The enabling act, however, was passed only after it was agreed that ward schooling would be publicly supported for the poor only and that provision for colleges should be dropped altogether. Was the university as actually organized in some sense a graduate institution? Jefferson's own testimony is ambiguous. In 1822, he spoke of existing colleges of the South as being preparatory to the university; but earlier he had talked of admitting students then going to Harvard, Princeton, Columbia, and the University of Pennsylvania. It would seem that the University of Virginia was the Southern and experimental counterpart of well-established colleges in the North.

The institutions designated generically as "colleges" play a puzzling role in the early projects. Plainly some authors were thinking of real institutions and their inadequacy as the highest schools of a federal republic, the proposition sometimes being that a university was needed as much to draw the ablest young men away from the localism of the existing colleges as to advance knowledge. Sometimes, however, "college" seems more a category, if not a catchall, than a level of concrete education. There was a gap between mastery of the three R's and Latin grammar at the beginning of education and the open-ended pursuit of knowledge in a university, and the college was to fill that space. It was as if many planners worked from the top of the system down, deductively, as it were, from what an ideal university required rather than upward, inductively, from the readiness for advanced study that completion of a concrete college course might provide. In short, the planners did not talk in terms of *graduate* education in the university: the chief significance of their work lies in the fact that they aimed high, although not in a clearly discernible anticipation of graduate education as we know it. Yet they were inclined to distinguish between college and university in a land where the terms had become almost interchangeable. That confusion of nomenclature had to be sorted out, but in light of what the existing college actually did, before the term *graduate* would have significance.

While interest in national planning ebbed, thought about the reshaping or founding of particular institutions began to flow. The change of tide is symbolized by a friendship that began between the aging Jefferson and the young George Ticknor when Ticknor visited Monticello before setting out for study abroad. Both men admired the cultivated mind; both were convinced that the country required educated leaders; both became academic reformers; both knew frustration. But their thoughts had different points of departure. Jefferson attempted to build a whole educational system according to a master plan; Ticknor confronted what he considered to be the defects of an existing undergraduate college—Harvard— with his experience as a university student abroad as a guide.

Ticknor studied in Germany, but he had not originally gone to the German university as to Mecca. Few Americans had studied there when Ticknor left home, and just before he did, he spoke of "the pools of stagnant learning in Germany and England" (Storr, 1953, p. 15). Once abroad, however, he discovered that although the vigorous spirit of youth had fled from England and although literature, his particular interest, was in a worse state in France and southern Europe, there was in Germany a spirit "of pursuing all literary studies philosophically—making scholarship as little of drudgery and mechanism as possible" (ibid., p. 16). As a student at Göttingen, he wanted to transplant that spirit to the United States. He was persuaded that the further progress of American learning depended upon a thoroughgoing revision of education and, while still abroad, he may have proposed—the record is incomplete—a faculty of philosophy at Harvard. President John T. Kirkland was sympathetic but remarked: "We are however poorer than you think." There was more in Kirkland's mind than that: the thought occurred to him, while considering Ticknor's argument, that Harvard might eventually become a gymnasium and a university; but his final judgment was that "to have a gymnasium & a University together on the same ground is not good" (ibid., p. 16). Both the comparison of the American college to the German gymnasium and the conclusion Kirkland came to would become stock themes in academic debate. After beginning service as a professor at Harvard, Ticknor himself underwent a change of heart. He was exempted from drudgery, but even so his experience was jolting. He still wished Harvard to be a university, but that did not seem immediately possible: "If we can ever have an University at Cambridge, which shall lead the intellectual character of the country, it can be I apprehend only when the present college shall have been settled into a thorough & well disciplined high school . . ." (ibid., p. 18). Ticknor's views attracted the support of several overseers, including Justice Joseph Story, and the reform movement that they put underway presently led to a revision of the regulations. The changes included the division of the college into departments and the recognition of some subjects, not indispensable for a degree, among which the student had a choice. These provisions could have opened the way for movement toward something more elevated than a high school; and indeed, in the midst of debate, Ticknor had taken heart sufficiently to modify his stringent recommendation that Harvard should first be made a good high school. He saw the possibility of finding "a beneficial compromise" between the old system and "the most liberal conception that would be demanded

by one of the really free and philosophical Universities of Europe"
(ibid., p. 19). The college should be considered a place where all
the branches of human knowledge would, at last, be taught. Thus
the reforms now remembered in connection with Ticknor's name
embodied a principle of organic growth—a growth not dependent
upon the definition of "college" and "university" as separate strata
of education. What mattered was the offering of a choice of studies
(later the "elective system") taught by men who severally professed
particular branches of knowledge. But Harvard was too poor for
much experimentation, and the promise of the program did not fire
the imagination of the faculty. The reformers had neglected to con-
sult with it fully; and at least one professor, Andrews Norton,
precisely ticked off the difficulty of Ticknor's compromise. Taken
as a whole, Norton argued, the plan did not seem to afford any
settled and distinct conception of the character that it was proposed to give the college: "Is it to be a University? One would think
that this should be gradually aimed at" (ibid., p. 22). Plainly that
was what Ticknor wanted; but his gifts did not include skill in
academic politics. (See also Tyack, 1967, pp. 85–128.)

Norton's views, as well as those of Stiles nearly a half-century
before, indicate the error of dismissing the men of the "old-fashioned" college simply as last-ditch conservatives who had to be
displaced before the university and graduate education could be
established. It is easier to find fault with the college mentality than
to do it justice. In 1827, Yale thought it necessary to respond to a
demand for reform that Ticknor's plan illustrates; and the report
that Yale issued in 1828 is now commonly accepted as the classic
defense of the old, prescribed curriculum that emphasized the
ancient languages in particular and discipline of broadly defined
"faculties" of mind in general. That is the central thrust of the
report; but in one of its parts, President Jeremiah Day looked beyond the undergraduate course. In words that say much about the
character of that course, Day sketched out the benefits a student
gained from its completion:

When the student has passed beyond the rugged and cheerless region of
elementary learning, into the open and enchanting field where the great
masters of science are moving onward with enthusiastic emulation; when,
instead of plodding over a page of Latin or Greek, with his grammars, and
dictionaries, and commentaries, he reads those languages with facility and
delight; when, after taking a general survey of the extensive and diversified

territories of literature, he has selected those spots for cultivation which are best adapted to his talents and taste; he may then be safely left to pursue his course, without the impulse of authoritative injunction, or regulation of statutes and penalties (Storr, 1953, pp. 30–31).

Day had in mind the idea of "a School of philosophy for the higher researches of literature and science," but he believed that the college resembled the German gymnasium and had its distinct and appropriate purpose. Perhaps Day was answering the son of his predecessor in office, Timothy Dwight. In 1825–26, Henry E. Dwight had written from Germany both of the superior classical education provided by the gymnasia and of four faculties, including the philosophical, into which the German university was divided. The older generation was agreeing with the younger but asking it to be patient. Day adumbrated a policy that was to stand as an alternative to Ticknor's conception of university building: The unitary, prescribed curriculum of the college should stand, but a faculty of philosophy should presently be erected above it. Within the terms of that view, cultivation of particular talents as distinct from the disciplining of the mind was the study appropriate for graduates — indeed graduate study. Day did not make shortage of money a hypocritical excuse for sticking to the status quo, for he was prepared to accept funds in support of graduate students. During Day's administration, Sheldon Clark, a successful Connecticut farmer with no family of his own, gave Yale $1,000 to be held as capital accumulating interest until 1848. The interest was then to be awarded as scholarships to students who resided in New Haven for two years just after graduation and studied in accord with their own bent and prospects of usefulness, the professions excluded. In 1849, the second Timothy Dwight, who was himself to become a President of Yale, received a Sheldon Clark scholarship (ibid., pp. 29–33, 56).

But however open the minds of some academics might be, the mode of instruction in the college was not designed to promote inquiry. Especially as the evangelical spirit gained momentum, piety took precedence over intellect. Indeed, it can be argued that the evangelicalism of the nineteenth century, in contrast to an earlier rationalism, worked to set back the development of advanced studies. True, a number of academics, notably the college presidents, had tough minds, strong opinions, and a gift for argument. The customary senior course in moral philosophy might be orthodox, but it was not flabby. The literary societies, around which extracurricular life revolved, fostered disputation, and their libraries allowed a student to escape from textbooks. The curriculum was prescribed, however, without regard to individual talents and taste, and in class, drill was more the rule than the exception: "The root of the matter," a Harvard instructor said, "is to be found in the humble and simple, old-school, tedious business of recitation" (ibid., p. 3). The furniture of the mind, in the language of the Yale report, consisted principally of the elements of conventional learning. The advancement of knowledge and the promotion of the disciplines appropriate to it, as distinct from mental discipline, were not the goals of the college (Schmidt, 1930; Smith, 1956, pp. 3–27; Harding, 1971).

Yet the curriculum, although prescribed, was not static, nor was it completely shielded from knowledge that was new and utilitarian. The difficulty was that four years offered too little time for mastery of new studies in addition to the old. Unless some topics were covered with only a lick and a promise, an alternative to ad hoc adjustment was required. Tucking new subjects in here and there meant only that the four-year curriculum would become increasingly cramped as the pressure of expanding knowledge increased. One possibility was to open up undergraduate education by offering several bachelor's degrees and by introducing vocational subjects and whatever else "the spirit of the age" demanded. Another possibility was to make more room for truly higher education by pushing up the ceiling on time spent in study. To describe this option, George Pierson has spoken of the horizontal and the vertical university. In the American situation, the school of thought favoring the vertical university pointed explicitly toward study after college graduation (Pierson, 1950, p. 73).

A model from Germany was not actually required, but one was tried at Harvard as the Ticknor reforms were petering out. In 1828 the *North American Review* had called attention to the inestimable benefit to the public resulting from the German philological "seminaries." Among other things they imparted to the student a scientific knowledge of the profession he was going to practice as a teacher, and they enabled him to instill into the tender mind of his pupil "those delicate and elevated feelings of honor, which are the best safeguard against illiberality of opinion, and against abuse of confidence" (Storr, 1953, pp. 24–25). In 1831, Charles Beck, a classicist with a Tübingen doctorate, came to Harvard and shortly proposed the establishment of a philological seminary designed to train teachers. That the idea was strange is suggested by the fact that a visiting committee substituted *philosophical* for *philological* to designate the seminary. It was Beck's proposal that instruction in the classical languages should not stop for students at the end of the junior year, as was the rule, but rather should continue for two or, if possible, three years; that instruction should be by lecture, with continual recourse to the sources; that the students should write dissertations and examinations; and that funds should be available for fifth- or sixth-year men. Beck referred to the receipt of "certificates" after examination, but he may have been thinking of the award of the Ph.D. as the goal. Also, he contemplated the eventual addition of mathematics to the program and thought ahead to a faculty of philosophy, hence, perhaps, the confusion over terms. A curriculum covering a year's work, presumably for seniors, was floated in 1831–32, but the plan gained no momentum and shortly disappeared. As Beck discovered, the vertical university required money that was not then forthcoming (ibid., pp. 24–28).

3. Dreams of the American University

The line between the vertical university and the horizontal university was not always as clear in actual planning at the time as it is in hindsight. The difference had to be worked out in debate, where the idea of wider service had its own impact upon the development of graduate education. The idea so gingered up the college that it looked increasingly less like a gymnasium, and it provided the device of the open lecture course, which gave promise of elevating study as well as accommodating it to more democratic, utilitarian times. When Beck launched the seminary in Cambridge, the currents of academic policy had already come together, for in 1830 there had been preliminary discussion on what was to be the University of the City of New York — now New York University. The earliest argument for the founding of a new university in the city ranged widely over the educational requirements of the time. Something was needed — in modern language — for commuting students in training for the learned professions; for young men preparing for agriculture, business, and engineering; for people already in those vocations who wanted adult education; for the elderly and the leisured who might study for pleasure; and for any Americans seeking a concentration of educational facilities. But what form should an urban university take? Anticipating the latter practice of philanthropic foundations, the promoters of the university called a "literary convention" or conference: the press called it a "Congress of Philosophers." European standards — and not of the same era — were well represented by the experience of the members. The aging Albert Gallatin had been educated in Geneva before immigrating to the United States — and had as a much younger man been Jefferson's Secretary of the Treasury; another member was the youthful Henry E. Dwight; two others, Joseph Leo Wolf and Ferdinand R. Hassler, superintendent of the Coastal Survey, were native Europeans who had just been arguing with each other in print over the nature of German university education. The sessions allowed a more comprehensive pooling of academic views than had probably occurred in the United States before. The topics of discussion were varied, including the question of open, public lectures and also that of how far the systems of the universities of Europe might be desirable institutions in the United States. Several speakers observed that the American colleges were not similar to European universities. Wolf spelled out the moral: "The principal point to be kept in view, is in my opinion, the distinct line, which should be drawn between a college and a University. . . . Both may exist under the same head, but separately from each other. But the question is: what is called for? is it a university, or a college? and what are the objects of each?" (Storr, 1953, p. 36). The one institution, Wolf said, fitted young men for the common vocations of life; the other was to satisfy the higher demands of science—and students there should be expected to have passed previously through a regular college education. The distinctiveness of a university as a graduate institution was thus driven home, as was the idea that university work would be fatally compromised if it were mixed with college study. Gallatin saw that two purposes were involved in the idea of the proposed university and neither purpose was conventionally collegiate. One was to elevate the standard of learning, to complete studies begun in the colleges, and to embrace branches not taught there—to create a university in the European sense of the word; the other was to diffuse knowledge and to render it more accessible to the community at large. The difference Gallatin had in mind was plainly that between the vertical and the horizontal universities (ibid., pp. 33–38).

The new university was organized to include two general departments, one to offer instruction in the higher branches and the other to offer complete courses, with and without the classics, at the lower level. The prospect of the higher department figured in the appeals made to the state on behalf of the university for a charter and later for a subsidy; and in 1835, three-year masters programs were announced for the faculties of letters and fine arts and of science and the arts (including architecture and engineering). But the higher department failed to mature. James M. Mathews, the president of the university, believed (correctly) that the university was designed to carry the student beyond the limits of the usual college course; but Mathews's actions gave little evidence that he felt a deep personal commitment to that part of the plan. He certainly proved incapable of getting on with professors who might have given momentum to graduate study. Then in the depression year of 1837, the university could aim only at an economy that would not debase the undergraduate work (ibid., pp. 39–43).

Much of the same counterpoint of discussion over the advancement and diffusion of knowledge that the New York plan had produced became the particular mark of debate over the bequest of James Smithson. The idea of a national university was revived in 1838 when the Secretary of State sought advice from experts in science and education. Thomas Cooper, who had discussed education with Jefferson, responded that a university open only to college graduates should be founded. The course should cover not less than three years and should provide such useful, not ornamental, studies as saved labor and multiplied comforts for the mass of mankind: the higher calculus yes; but no mere literature— "Things, not words" (ibid., p. 44). Another academic, President Francis Wayland of Brown, argued for a level of education between college and professional training, i.e., a kind of graduate education that was still not the highest education. Degrees should be earned through study, and the graduate should be allowed to teach for ticket-fees, a practice that would stimulate the regular professors and train teachers. Neither plan (obviously) was adopted by Congress, but unlike earlier proposals for a national university, these plans contemplated the use of money-in-hand—something *was* founded. The game of might-have-beens lends itself to fatuity, but speculation on the Smithson case has some heuristic value. The adoption of the omnibus term Smithsonian *Institution* was the appropriate outcome of a debate in which a wide range of possibilities from popular education to promotion of high scholarship were put forward. Had the latitude of its title been exploited to justify in-service training of apprentice scientists and teachers of science at a time when the colleges were not heavily committed in that direction, an incentive that was shortly to begin working powerfully for academic reform in the colleges might have been diminished and the venue of what became advanced education in science might have been changed (ibid., pp. 43–45).

It was not accidental that the Smithsonian Institution emphasized scientific work in something like the modern sense of the term. The sciences were growing vigorously in the middle years of the century and the scientists labored to secure unhedged institutional recognition for their work: Joseph Henry, first head of the Smithsonian Institution, was but one of a number of Americans who explored not only nature but the ways to make investigating it a profession. Not long after the Smithsonian was under way, Harvard and Yale felt the impact of such concerns as Henry had. Scientific studies were no novelty at either institution, but at neither college did the provision for science satisfy the scientists. At both, too, the amplification of the program in the interest of science was associated with a general effort to elevate the ceiling of studies. In his inaugural address as President of Harvard in 1846, Edward Everett asked whether the time had not arrived when the Harvard system should be expanded in two directions by establishing a philosophical faculty, with a view to the completion of liberal education, and by organizing a school of theoretical and practical science. (Everett savored a new name for Harvard, the University at Cambridge.) Unlike his sometime colleague, George Ticknor, Everett solicited faculty opinion on his ideas, including an earned master's degree. Favorable comment arrived at the president's desk from faculty members in both the sciences and the humanities; and Everett sat down to make plans with Benjamin Peirce, the Perkins Professor of Astronomy and Mathematics, who had for several years been arguing for the establishment of a scientific school. Peirce feared the opposition of an "uncompromising conservatism [of some alumni], which is disposed to claim for every blockhead, who is a graduate of three years standing, a vested right to the title of master of arts," and so suggested the establishment of a new and independent school for instruction in the higher departments of learning (ibid., p. 48). What Peirce had in mind was a distinct school of practical and theoretical science that would serve, among others, college graduates who wished either to study science generally (presumably not as prospective experts) or to perfect themselves in any of its branches. The school would also offer French, German, history, geography, and rhetoric. Thus it would provide graduate instruction without being strictly a graduate school in our sense and would give science its own home without being wholly scientific. The apparent anomalies in the proposal can be best explained by reference to Peirce's disgust with conservatism: several kinds of needed reform could be combined in a school beyond the reach of the diehards.

As organized, the new department was amorphous and was regarded as an experiment without a fixed character. With the appointment of two humanists to the faculty of the department, it was not exclusively scientific. The president could write: "Although we call it 'Scientific', we have made provisions for Students of Classical learning . . ." (ibid., p. 50). As a young man, Everett had understood that the European universities were professional schools preparing young men for teaching as well as other careers; and, as president, he noticed especially that higher training in philological and classical learning would yield accomplished teachers. The elements of a graduate school of arts and sciences can be read back into the possibilities that the new department revealed. Soon, however, the philanthropist Abbott Lawrence would declare his intention to make the then extraordinarily large gift of $50,000 for support of scientific education at Harvard. It was Everett's expectation that the entire organization of the department would merge in—i.e., be submerged by—the Lawrence endowment, and the new department, named the Lawrence Scientific School, did cease to be a general graduate school even in embryo. Although Everett wanted the philological side of the work to survive in announcements, he gave way to the opinion that nonscientific work in the school should be suspended for the time being. It was never revived, and Everett had to content himself with observing in 1849, after his resignation as president, that the scientific faculty as originally organized, and including professors of Greek and Latin, might have been considered to form, with the professional schools, an institution closely resembling the universities of Europe, especially those of Germany. But Everett had not been the president to fight for the actuality suggested by that inflated comparison (ibid., pp. 17, 49–53).

The classicist, Charles Beck, regretted that the department had been named "Scientific School" and remarked: "Yale College, which has lately established a similar department, has been more fortunate in the selection of its name, calling it Department of Philosophy and the Arts" (ibid., p. 51). Yale, too, inaugurated a new president, Theodore D. Woolsey, in 1846. Like Everett, he had known German university education at first hand. Woolsey looked forward to the time when a school of natural sciences should attract students who had finished their college course, but he was not simply interested in expansion of scientific work. Before his inauguration, a school of science had been proposed for Yale, chiefly by Benjamin Silliman, Professor of Chemistry, Pharmacy, Mineralogy, and Geology; and Woolsey suggested that the scheme should be

broadened to provide advanced instruction in nonscientific subjects. In 1847, a committee recommended the establishment of a
Department of Philosophy and the Arts that embraced the humanities, the moral sciences (or the protosocial sciences), and the natural sciences, including their applications. From time to time, the
committee remarked, new branches of study were called for by the
public, but if they were added to the undergraduate course, they
would crowd it and interfere with its purpose as a training ground
—the discipline of the mind again. (At Harvard, Everett remarked
that the scientific school was a means of throwing off from the
college proper some of the branches of study then pursued super-
ficially by undergraduates who were frittering away time much
better employed on "the standard academical studies.") Also, the
Yale committee advised, the opportunities arising from the Berkeley
and Sheldon Clark scholarships would be the greater if recipients
were provided with formal instruction and not left to themselves.
The latter scholarships were shortly to become available, and Yale,
the committee thought, was likely to have more scholarships (Storr,
1953, pp. 53–57; Furniss, 1965, pp. 1–23). In 1848, Charles Astor
Bristed, a grandson of John Jacob Astor and a Yale graduate who
studied at Cambridge University, did establish a scholarship to be
held by the recipient until he would regularly take his M.A. degree.
Four years later, Bristed published *Five Years in an English University,* a book that indicates that, long before graduate education
flourished, the graduate fellowship was explicitly prescribed—
and in Bristed's case, provided—as a necessary tonic for American
higher education. Bristed believed that the greatest failing of the
American colleges was a lack of specific endowments to support
as well as encourage learning: "As for resident Graduates wishing
to pursue some literary or philosophical faculty beyond the college
course, there is no provision for them whatever [untrue of Yale],
nor any opening beyond the comparatively small number of Professorships and Tutorships." It was Bristed's emphatic judgment:
"We want endowments" (Storr, 1953, pp. 65–66).

The Yale Corporation approved the committee's recommendation, and the new department was announced for 1847–48. Graduation from college was not required of students, but those in
philology and mathematics were warned that they must be well
grounded, and some graduates, including the second Timothy
Dwight, did enroll. Part of the studies offered, such as elementary
chemistry and applications of science to agriculture, fall outside

the limits of the modern graduate school—and indeed the announce-ment did not swing upon a distinction between graduate and under-graduate levels—but Dwight at least found that reading Thucydides and Pindar with President Woolsey was stimulating beyond any-thing he had known as an undergraduate. His two years in the department were, Dwight recalled, the most valuable of his educa-tion. It would be nit-picking to argue that Yale was not engaged in offering something very like graduate work.

The new departments at Harvard and Yale bore a remarkable resemblance to each other in origins and early plan. Both adum-brated graduate studies in the arts and sciences but at the same time represented a somewhat indeterminate experiment in the horizontal expansion of higher education to serve persons or offer studies classifiable as neither undergraduate in the then conven-tional sense nor graduate in our developed sense. One is reminded of Frederick William Maitland's comment apropos of the law re-flected in Domesday Book: "Simplicity [of idea] is the outcome of technical subtlety; it is the goal not the starting point. As we go backwards the familiar outlines become blurred; the ideas become fluid, and instead of the simple we find the indefinite" (Maitland, 1921, p. 9). The Lawrence gift to Harvard meant, however, a part-ing of the ways. For more than two decades, Harvard's course led for part of the time away from systematic graduate education and for the rest of the time into alleys that turned out to be blind, while Yale moved toward a graduate program with a familiar outline, in our terms. The steps that Yale took were usually measured, but in 1856, James D. Dana, the Silliman Professor of Natural History, let his imagination run free. The potentiality of the Depart-ment of Philosophy and Arts excited him. With only a little wider expansion of the scheme, it would cover the highest branches of literary and scientific education, adapted to carry forward the graduate of the college through a full university system of studies. Apparently taking it for granted that the scientific side of the de-partment was already strong, Dana argued that if courses were arranged in general history, philology, etc.—the humanistic side—"the number of resident graduates would greatly increase, and a new era [would] dawn upon American learning." His question was: "Why not have here, THE AMERICAN UNIVERSITY!" (Storr, 1953, p. 57).

Both the idea and the rhetoric belonged exactly to the moment. In the decade after 1850, the idea of a federally supported university, crowning a national system of schools, a national university in the old sense, had little more influence upon the thinking of Americans than it had had for years; nevertheless, they spoke passionately of the university that would be American. In that decade, many men, planning for many sites, set about to reform this or that college drastically or to create a wholly new institution that would be, emphatically, a university. Projects multiplied, and a kind of exaltation often set the key. Indeed Henry P. Tappan's mode of expression was described as being "oracular." In 1851, before becoming president of the University of Michigan, he argued for the building of a university in New York City. (Earlier he had been a professor at the University of the City of New York, and his writing may be read as indirect commentary upon its short-comings.) Education had, Tappan said, four levels—the primitive or practical, the artistic and aesthetic, the professional, and the "ideal or philosophical," which the university alone could develop adequately:

Here the capacities of the mind are considered, and the system of education is shaped simply for *educating*—leading forth—unfolding these capac-ities. We now leave out of view the mere utilities of life, the demands of particular arts, the preparations of a particular profession. We ask, what man is—what he is capable of becoming? We find him endowed with high powers of thought, observation and reasoning—with imagination and taste —with conscience and moral determination. And in all these he is capable of growing indefinitely—of becoming more and more intellectual, more and more beautiful in his imaginative and tasteful functions—more wise and good, without an assignable limit (ibid., p. 61).

If preoccupation with the transcendent and the boundless is a mark of romanticism, that was romantic academicism. Perhaps Tappan *was* oracular, but, as modern liberals have been advised to do, he preached what he practiced.

It was a time of cultural patriotism and academic aspirations, and the two often merged. Although the planners sometimes spoke for the greater glory of particular institutions or in support of par-ticular disciplines, it is not always possible to draw a sharp line between special pleading and the larger view in which building a university was a way to focus, express, and elevate the life of the nation. The American university—the definite article was used frequently—would be, as it were, the institutional counterpart of the American scholar, whose coming Ralph Waldo Emerson had prophesied. As a goal that had to be reached, the Great American University stood beside the Great American Poem.

The objects the planners had in mind were not altogether new. James D. Dana was picking up an old theme when he argued, in behalf of a fully developed Department of Philosophy and the Arts at Yale, that only when it had become a realized fact could youth be prevented "from seeking in the atmosphere of Germany the knowledge for which they yearn" (ibid., p. 57). It had long been feared that young Americans would breathe in corruption abroad even as they acquired the learning available only there. The planning of the decade also betrays impatience with the reputed inferiority of American culture, but smarting at the thought of cultural colonialism had begun long since. What particularly characterizes the 1850s was the confident framing of large plans, to provide a concentration of resources in preparation for an intellectual thrust upward. Alexander D. Bache struck the keynote in 1856 while addressing an organization that sponsored expositions. Speaking as if he were a guide, Bache provided an inventory of the institutions that America could exhibit. The schools, academies, colleges, mechanics institutes, government projects, and astronomical observatories, although good in themselves, were not sufficient to the great end of organizing intelligence: "Where is our American University?" (ibid., pp. 57, 89–91).

In retrospect, it is plain that organization was in fact needed. Even as colonials, the Americans had created more institutions with the power to grant degrees than existed in the mother country; after independence, the recognition of the sovereign right of states to charter corporations produced what amounted to an American variant of academic freedom, i.e., virtually free incorporation of degree-granting institutions. Some states, notably Michigan, attempted to establish central control of higher education, but the tendency of legislatures was to act, in effect, upon the presumption that the burden of proof lay with the opponents, not the supporters, of petitions for charters. Institutions were founded in numbers that were monstrously large by British and continental standards. Although the mortality rate resembled that for bankruptcies in business, many institutions survived, if frequently in poverty. (See Tewksbury, 1932.) The result was that for students, college education was geographically more available than it would otherwise have been, but for the professors, the possibility of day-to-day collaboration was slight. Perhaps with the railroads in mind, Benjamin Peirce proposed a university that would embrace "the greatest variety" and the resources of many localities by building a faculty on part-time appointment with professors living wherever they pleased: "All the powerful minds of the country can be concentrated upon this institution. . . ." (Storr, 1953, p. 90). Bache described the alternative solution:

There is a great and growing demand in our country for something higher than college instruction; and one great University, if fairly set in motion, would thrive. . . . For the sake of being together, I know that the leading scientific men of the country, with few exceptions, . . . would leave their present homes. . . . There are men enough to make one very brilliant institution by their high qualities and learning (ibid., p. 68).

The problem was to find financial support. It was not accidental that perhaps the most active and distinguished group of planners, the Lazzaroni, took its name from the Italian beggars. Both Peirce and Bache belonged to the Lazzaroni, and a number of other scientists were members of the club or were in touch with it: James D. Dana, mineralogy; Benjamin A. Gould, Jr., astronomy; Josiah D. Whitney, mineralogy; James Hall, geology and paleontology; Oliver Wolcott Gibbs, chemistry; and Louis Agassiz, biology. Samuel B. Ruggles, a layman interested in the advancement of science and higher education, also belonged to the club. The members could write back and forth lightheartedly; but they shared two very serious and cognate purposes—the building of a university and the creation of a national academy to advance and control the scientific work conducted under the auspices of the federal government. Their plans did not depend upon federal support of the university, but they did foreshadow the linkage of advanced studies and graduate work with the formation of an integrated national policy in regard to science. In their search for money to support a university, they went to Albany where Hall served as superintendent of the New York geographical survey and where the efforts they made helped to inspire some local and legislative sentiment in favor of a university. Referring to his earlier activity in behalf of internal improvements, Ruggles in effect harked back to an old argument for a national university. He also picked up the argument of the Lazzaroni: The friends of the new university proposed "to unite and combine in one mass, a body of learned men, far exceeding in number and strength anything that has yet been presented to the

American world" (ibid., p. 70). The established colleges had a place, but something broader and more diversified was needed to enable the student to pursue specialized knowledge to its most extreme limits.[1]

But, in Whitney's phrase, the university at Albany fizzled out; and the Lazzaroni turned toward New York City, where in 1855, Bache put the case that a university should not only diffuse knowledge:

> . . . it must lead in the advancement of science through the researches of its professors. . . . Pupils should not only resort to it to learn what had passed into the books of the day, but what had been discovered by its teachers themselves. The living account of active research would thus inspire the pupils, and the professors would have not only hearers but followers (ibid., p. 83).

But for *pupils,* such words would become a part of academic liturgy. Earlier in the same year, and also in New York City, Tappan argued that universities should be urban—and doubtless he meant New York; for cities possessed wealth and facilitated what he called the fellowship of congenial spirits necessary to scholars. He was speaking the language of the scientists, and in 1855–56, he joined forces with the Lazzaroni, who called him "General," in an effort to create in New York a combined university and academy of sciences and arts—a "union" as the matter was put to Peter Cooper. The benefaction which he was just then contemplating would be incorporated into the university, which would also be connected with the Astor Library. (Its head, Joseph G. Cogswell, had explored the German universities when Ticknor and Everett had.) The Free Academy (later City College) and Columbia would be colleges of the university. The union could attract private subscriptions and appropriations from the city (ibid., pp. 82–85).

Again a grand project aborted, but for both Tappan and Ruggles, advocacy of new universities was an interlude in the reform of existing institutions. As president of the University of Michigan, Tappan had in 1854 looked forward to the time when lectures would extend beyond those then given undergraduates. In 1856, after collapse of the New York project, he reported to the Michigan

[1] For discussion of the Lazzaroni, see Lurie, 1960, pp. 180–184, 323–325; Thompson, 1946; Dupree, 1964, pp. 118, 135–142.

regents: "The graduate of a College is not prepared to become a College Professor. But the direct object of a University is to prepare men to teach in the University itself, or in any other institution" (ibid., pp. 114–115). These statements were but part of an effort to elevate the University of Michigan, and in 1858 it launched master's-degree programs that provided a number of courses and required the writing of a thesis. The plan, however, had little chance to mature, as Tappan shortly resigned (Donnelly, et al., 1953, vol. 3, pp. 1037–1039).

Ruggles's base was Columbia College, of which he was an energetic trustee. From 1852, he worked pertinaciously to transform it into Columbia University. Before the professional scientist Bache had spoken of the university and research in New York, the lay trustee had written a pamphlet in which he not only equated the college and the gymnasium but argued for a university where the student might pursue any path he chose to its limit and where above all "original research and discovery by the ablest men the world can furnish, shall add daily to the great sum of human knowledge" (Storr, 1953, p. 97). Ruggles had some support locally, and a Committee of Inquiry received outside advice in favor of the university idea; but the board moved slowly. Then, in 1857, it voted a reorganization of the undergraduate program and the creation of postgraduate schools of science, letters, and jurisprudence. The student would pursue a unitary course for three years and then as a senior would choose between departments corresponding to the postgraduate schools. After graduation, the student would qualify for the M.A. degree following a minimum of two years of advanced work. Once organized, however, the schools of letters and science languished from a lack of students. Ruggles's son-in-law, George T. Strong, described the situation with characteristic cynicism: "This people is not ripe for higher education. . . . Could we afford to lay out $10,000 per annum in stipends to clever young men and hire a dozen best graduate students every year to stay in college and be pumped into, we might accomplish something." Yet Strong believed that in perishing the plan might just possibly leave a germ surviving "whence there may be natural development and expansion hereafter" (ibid., pp. 107, 111).

Hope deferred was the bare result of much planning in the decade. At the University of Pennsylvania, Bishop Alonzo Potter unsuccessfully advocated that the institution should become an "open University" where college graduates and other young men bent upon gaining knowledge could have the teaching of the best masters. Union College attempted to create a higher faculty and a fellowship system. And the University of the South was put under way with an M.A. program, a fellowship system, and promise of receiving substantial endowment—but too late. More than a half-century of debate and experiment had not produced an institution that either challenged the hegemony of the college in higher education or created a demand for graduate education. Its form, if it was to exist at all, remained in doubt. Yet the need, as distinct from the demand, for graduate education, had been declared loudly and repeatedly: a cause had been created, and it had been related to a variety of profoundly moving interests. Finally, in 1860, Yale instituted the Ph.D. degree—and awarded it in 1861 to three candidates (ibid., pp. 74–81, 118–124).

4. The Rise of the American University and the Ph.D. Degree

In the history of American higher education, it seems inevitable that the period after 1861 should be called the age of the universities. They monopolized neither the initiative nor the power in higher education, but they did become preeminent there and in research as well. Before 1861, no foreign observer of American society would have reported that the university, as distinct from the college, existed except in name; but by the turn of the century, the question would have been how the American university compared with one or another prototype abroad. The American university, like the British, embraced the college, but its characteristic feature was a graduate school with a Ph.D. program. When we discuss other degrees beyond the bachelor's—say the M.A., Ed.D., and the teaching doctorate—we are inclined to locate them in the scheme of things by indicating how the course toward them approaches or deviates from that for the Ph.D. degree. In retrospect we might suppose that the institution of the Ph.D. at Yale was the point of no return in the history of American graduate education. Yet the establishment of the Ph.D. degree occurred by stages.

Three students took the Yale Ph.D. degree in 1861, three in 1862, and only one in 1863, but the stream continued. The original requirements were that candidates should devote two years of study to two distinct departments of learning in the Department of Philosophy and the Arts, should pass a final examination, and should present a thesis proving high attainments in their studies. It was not stipulated that such attainment should be in the realm of original research; nor was it indicated that writing of the thesis should occupy the candidate for at least a year after completion of the two required years of study. Yet something like graduate study as we know it was taking shape. In 1875, William Harper, an

18-year-old graduate of Muskingum College and later first president of the University of Chicago, took a Yale Ph.D. after writing a thesis on prepositions in Latin, Greek, Sanskrit, and Gothic. It was no longer absolutely necessary for the gifted young American to seek his doctorate abroad. As early as 1869, the year in which he became president of Harvard, Charles W. Eliot did justice to both the fact and the mood of university building at Yale: the department was a legitimate success "on a really high level, if also on a modest scale." The existence of the program, "unpretentious but genuine, and perseveringly offered to a few real students," helped to prove that there was a demand for instruction higher than that of the ordinary college course and yet different from that of the law, medical, and theological schools (Storr, 1953, p. 58). The terms Eliot used to define the demand have significance. He did not speak generically of a "graduate school of arts and sciences" but rather he defined the kind of instruction he had in mind by specifying what did not provide it. Neither the decades of discussion before institution of the Ph.D. degree nor the first successes with it had given graduate education in arts and sciences a distinctive meaning and a commonly acknowledged hallmark (Furniss, 1965, p. 18; Storr, 1953, p. 57–58).

Eliot's thought fits into a pattern that had been developing somewhat interruptedly at Harvard over 20 years. The reforms of the 1840s had been partly inspired by the intentions of scientists, and a resurgence of interest in university building at Harvard had its beginning, in 1861, in an effort to reform instruction in the Scientific School, of which the young Eliot was an officer. Some of the faces were not new; Louis Agassiz and Benjamin Peirce began to plan again. The Lazzaroni found an ally in Thomas Hill, president of Harvard, whose mind Peirce described as Alps on Alps.[1] The Yale report of 1828 would not have left Hill cold. He believed that "a generous culture of every faculty" was a necessary foundation (Hill, 1863, p. 27), but he also believed that specialization at the highest level of education was necessary, too. As each student was peculiarly fitted by nature for a particular kind of work, the greatest achievement of education was the development to the highest degree of "the particular talent and genius" of the individual student, to enable him to do his work in the most efficient and thorough manner possible (ibid., p. 24). Given the rapid

[1] Peirce to A. D. Bache, February 5, 1863, in Benjamin Peirce papers, Harvard University.

expansion of knowledge, nobody could expect to master the entire body of science and art; hence a need for advanced, graduate education. Hill looked ahead to "some possible career . . . more distinctly philosophical and literary than any now free to our young graduates" (ibid., p. 36). The new education should aid B.A.'s in the pursuit of the true, the beautiful, and the good. It would be specialized, but not vocational in the sense that existing professional education was:

Our Divinity School prepares its scholars to take charge of parishes; but where are our young men coming simply as lovers of truth, simply as scholars, for aid in exploring the highest realms of human thought? Our Law School prepares young gentlemen, after a certain course, for admission to the bar; but are any of our younger graduates studying jurisprudence as a science; led simply by the love of its dignified beauty. Our Medical School prepares young men to enter into practice; even our Scientific School is largely technological, teaching the applications of science as much as science itself (ibid., p. 36–37).

As Eliot would later, Hill was defining what should be done by reference to what remained when the limits of professional education were reached. Yet the ideal was positive; it was exemplified by the observatory and the zoological museum, "in which the glory of the Creator and general welfare of mankind are generally recognized as the prominent ends, without reference to the pecuniary advantages which individual students shall reap from their acquirements" (ibid., pp. 36–37). Hill was approaching—but had not quite reached—the idea of the graduate school as the place where the pursuit of truth for its own sake is institutionalized: it had to be described in terms of what it was not. It was itself a place where disinterested and open-ended inquiry could make the hitherto shapeless contents of mind into disciplines sufficiently intelligible to be given names.

The specific device of instruction that Harvard adopted, following Agassiz' lead, consisted of university lectures, open to members of the professional schools, teachers, and others, as well as to graduates of colleges. Some of the lectures reached a high level— Peirce spoke of a course he gave on space described mathematically as "transcendentalism in three dimensions"[2]—and some graduate students did attend lectures. Hill was partially satisfied; and his

[2] Peirce to A. D. Bache, November 1, 1863, in Benjamin Peirce papers, Harvard University.

successor, Eliot, gave his support to university lecturing. Similarly, at Cornell University, which had opened just a year before Eliot's inauguration in 1869, President Andrew D. White launched a series of university lectures, as part of an effort to aid—as he recalled later—"in founding and building a worthy American university" (Becker, 1943, p. 66).

White had studied abroad after graduating from Yale and before joining Henry P. Tappan's faculty at the University of Michigan, and he came to Ithaca with that dream. White and Eliot were of the same genus within the emerging species of academic man. They owed nothing to the clerical tradition of academic preferment; and by education and appointment they were identified, early in adult life, with the new, expanding learning—White with history and Eliot with natural science. Both had, however, the minds of men of affairs and were drawn toward administration and away from professional careers. Both were university builders. True, Eliot's style was more astringent than White's. It was Eliot who said in 1873: "There is something childish in this uneasy hankering for a big university in America, as there is also in that impatient longing for a distinctive American literature which we so often hear expressed" (Storr, 1953, p. 131). Yet it was the tempo, not the goal of university building, about which Eliot was restrained: "It cannot be said too loudly or too often, that no subject of human inquiry can be out of place in the programme of a real university. It is only necessary that every subject should be taught at the university on a higher plane than elsewhere. . . . It is impossible to be too catholic in this matter" (Eliot, 1869, p. 215). Yet neither Eliot nor White began university building with the primary intention of creating a graduate faculty of the arts and sciences that would prepare students to take the Ph.D. degree. They did not conceive of Ph.D. work as an indispensable engine of academic reform —as the program that a president could slight only at the risk of leaving his institution something less than a university. The state of mind of academics in the early 1870s is thrown into relief by the case of the University of Chicago in the early 1890s. Before it opened, the friends of the university argued sharply over the speed with which it should grow from college to university stature; once it was decided that it should be a university from the beginning, a Ph.D. program was immediately instituted as if no alternative was thinkable. Opening in 1876, Johns Hopkins had given the American Ph.D. momentum.

The history of Johns Hopkins as a graduate school began before the opening, when the trustees sounded opinion on possible courses the university might follow: under the terms of a will made by the Baltimore financier, Johns Hopkins, the trustees had carte blanche beyond the stipulation that half of the $7 million estate should be used to found a university. They could decide what that meant. In particular, the trustees sought the advice of Eliot, White, and James B. Angell, president of the University of Michigan. White alone dealt sympathetically with a suggestion that the trustees should strike out immediately toward graduate study, but he did not press the argument. The three advisors did unite, however, in advising the trustees that Daniel C. Gilman, then president of the University of California, should be called to Baltimore. So it was that the Johns Hopkins represented the conjunction, for the first time, of a venturesome board, a substantial amount of un-committed capital, and a president who was ready to devote a major part of his energy and thought, as well as a major part of the income of the university, to the establishment of graduate studies in fields other than the existing professions. The Hopkins reform of medical education began well after that work had been established. Indeed, in the view of Hugh Hawkins, historian of the early Johns Hopkins University, the graduate program in the arts and sciences had begun to lose momentum in 1889 or before the medical school and hospital had been founded. So for a little more than a decade the Johns Hopkins University demonstrated what a heavy concentration of mind, resources, and will upon grad-uate education in the arts and sciences could do. The university provided an actual—and highly attractive—example of a research-oriented institution with a Ph.D. program supported by fellow-ships. Gilman, a Yale graduate and sometime officer of its depart-ment of Philosophy and the Arts, converted—it may be said—what had been a serious but still ancillary program in New Haven into the central activity of the university in Baltimore (Hawkins, 1960).

As Hawkins amply demonstrates, it was neither a kind of onto-logical purity as graduate education nor fidelity to the German model that made the Johns Hopkins University an acknowledged success. Its history did not prove, as one tradition had it, that grad-uate education was essentially different from undergraduate educa-tion and could not succeed if the two were linked together: an undergraduate curriculum was offered from the beginning. As to the German example: although it had its effect, a number of faculty members had been educated and had conducted their work under the inspiration of ideas that were not patently German (Holt, 1938, pp. 10–11). Nor did Gilman identify the idea of a university solely with specialized professional research in particular disciplines. In his *First Annual Report,* Gilman emphasized the role of the professor as investigator engaged in research; however he also asserted, with a hierarchical choice of adjectives: "In the universities teaching is essential, research important. . ." (Hawkins, 1960, p. 64). There are unresolved chords in the early history of the university, and not the least of these is that it inspired skepticism about the identification of the Ph.D. with monographic research. However, Johns Hopkins did provide a demonstration of Ph.D. study that was aggressive, exciting, and central to the meaning of the university.

One imagines an early Hopkins' Ph.D. saying—in Lincoln Steffens language—"I have been over into the future, and it works." Although much about the early Johns Hopkins University now seems to belong to a quaint period piece, it does not require a flight of fancy to comprehend the pattern of experience at the Hopkins: the student graduated from college, entered a community devoted largely, although not exclusively, to research, attended a seminar in a chosen field, perhaps won a fellowship, did research for a thesis, took a Ph.D., and looked forward to a professional career in an academic post. But would that pattern be familiar today if the trustees appointed under the terms of Johns Hopkins's will had accepted the bulk of the advice they received and had not opted to create the institution that was actually established? Did they truly shape the future by making the choice they did, in the sense that American graduate education would have been substantially different today if they had chosen differently; or did they simply anticipate a future in which the expansion of knowledge, the demands of an increasingly complex society, the accumulation of philanthropic capital, and much else was bound, sooner or later, to produce the kind of graduate education that the early Johns Hopkins University successfully attempted and that we are inclined to take for granted? The question, which involves classic issues in the philosophy of history, requires no definitive answer here, but the complexity of the situation out of which the question arises constitutes a *prima facie* case against any pat explanation of the direction taken by graduate education in the United States. Although President Eliot paid tribute to the Johns Hopkins University for the great influence it had exercised upon American higher education, it is no more possible to measure the specific impact of the university exactly than to quantify the effect of a seminal book. It seems safe to say, however, that the Johns Hopkins University put other institutions on their mettle. Given financial support for a distinguished faculty, a number of fellowships, publication of journals, and the other elements of the university, a graduate program did not have to grow slowly on the Yale model, nor did it have to be conducted as an adjunct or offshoot of a college program. Experience at the Johns Hopkins University suggests that a teaching device—the seminar—designed explicitly for graduate instruction was far more effective than such devices as the "university lecture," designed to facilitate both the vertical and the horizontal extension of the college. Also, the Johns Hopkins University converted many of its students to the belief that true academic life was what they had known in Baltimore: hence the Johns Hopkins University contributed, by sending out virtual missionaries, to the establishment of a particular standard. It is striking that one of the most acid of critics that the American university has had, Abraham Flexner, studied at the Johns Hopkins University and tested other institutions against it—to leave them smarting.

In the last quarter of the nineteenth century, a number of institutions rose above the horizon of collegiate instruction either as new universities or with the establishment of graduate education in existing colleges. The development of graduate education in such colleges consisted either of the strengthening of programs already in being, as at Yale, or of the growth of a new program in ground already prepared by the elective system and the elevation of undergraduate courses, as at Harvard—or of renewed effort where an old program had become moribund, as at Columbia. Not every project succeeded: at Bowdoin a graduate program was projected as early as 1871, only to be dropped. Programs of instruction might be launched before full-scale graduate schools as such were organized; thus graduate education sometimes moved toward full stature administratively only over a period of years. In two of the new universities, Clark and Chicago, graduate education was planned as a major effort from the beginning; indeed, at Clark the graduate program *was* the university for many years. No single formula governed the building of graduate schools. The structures designed for the government and administration of graduate education differed from university to university; and, while the esprit de corps of academics interested in graduate studies gave a fresh meaning to the old idea of a university as the community of scholars, the founding of a graduate school could give rise to controversy, even among its advocates. The classic case occurred in the beginning of the new century when Dean Andrew F. West and President Woodrow Wilson of Princeton fell into bitter and nearly disastrous conflict over a proposal to build a residential college of graduate studies—the symbol of community. In the professoriate at large, as Laurence R. Veysey has documented, a number of dissenters refused in the name of liberal culture to be reconciled to the values with which they associated graduate study. Its not-at-all-loyal opposition is ancient (Bragdon, 1967, pp. 353–383; Link, 1947, pp. 61–90; Wertenbaker, 1946, pp. 370–383; Veysey, 1965, p. 180 ff.).

THE FORCE OF THE PH.D. DEGREE Yet the creation of graduate schools continued, and a sense of common interest grew. While graduate study itself was just beginning to gather momentum, students organized a national federation of graduate clubs, published a handbook, and asked for uniform standards. Also, among the universities as institutions the rise of the Ph.D. programs was followed by a movement toward association and the standardization of requirements. Even before formal machinery to accomplish those purposes had been devised, emulation and migration had worked to keep Ph.D. degree programs in sight of each other. The Ithaca men who joined William R. Harper at Chicago brought the Cornell catalog with them. The universities were never entirely isolated from each other, if for no other reason than that they needed the same kind of talent and sought it in the same pool. Indeed rivalry over appointments began as early as Gilman's effort to build a faculty at the Johns Hopkins University. His gift for discovering the promise of young men may have been essential to its success, and not simply one reason for it, because there was no glut of scholars fit to be university professors and other institutions had their attractions. Thus Gilman could not lure Wolcott Gibbs, a sometime member of the Lazzaroni, away from his Rumford chair at Harvard. The situation of the universities resembled that of many contemporary business firms, which competed with each other and yet shared the same worries. Neither complete isolation nor complete consolidation served the purpose. Just at the turn of the century, the organization of the Association of American Universities (AAU) meant formal recognition of a need to explore—in the words of the presidents—matters of common interest relating to graduate study. The international reputation of the American Ph.D. degree was one of those matters, the first on the agenda, but the creation of a single great American university was not. Almost simultaneously with the foundation of the association, several of the presidents collaborated under other auspices to throw cold water upon an effort, led by John W. Hoyt, to found a national university. For years since he had served as American Commissioner at the Paris Exposition of 1867, Hoyt had sought to bring life and money to the idea. His work inspired one supporter, James H. Baker, president of the University of Colorado, to revive the rhetoric of an earlier age:

I mean by a national university a great post-graduate institution—a [university] greater than Berlin—wonderfully equipped, with professors representing the culture and the progress of the world, with thousands of graduate students from all parts of the country and from all countries of the world, standing as an ideal interest of Congress and of the American people, in touch with the people, and helping the people come to a consciousness of the true ideals of democracy, and spreading those ideals over the civilized world (Baker, 1901, p. 471).

The answer was that *the* American university was not needed: a group of truly national universities existed. That view has obviously prevailed, with the result that the regulation of graduate education has not come about through the fiat of an institution that could be called the standard university of the United States: graduate education would be a theme with variations. But the form of the theme would be heavily influenced by the Ph.D., recognized as the dominant chord. The organization of the AAU marked the establishment of the cognate ideas that what defined a university was the offering of graduate work and that what completed it, in essence as well as in time, was the granting of Ph.D. degrees (Berelson, 1960, pp. 16–17).

That definition did not mean that the university and the college became separate worlds. As George E. Peterson (1964, pp. 27–51) has indicated in reference to New England colleges, college presidents and others were prompted by the rise of the universities to insist upon the importance of educating the whole man, emphatically in the college, and a university man could look at the college with much condescension. Sympathies between college and university were imperfect; but the old principle—inspired by a com-

parison of the American college and the German *gymnasium*—
that college and university should be kept completely apart was
becoming a museum piece before the AAU was organized. Woodrow Wilson, at Princeton, struck the appropriate note: The idea
overshadowing all others in his mind was that "there should be a
constant, conscious, intimate action, interaction, and reaction
between graduates and undergraduates in the organization of a
university" (Link, 1947, p. 80). At the University of Chicago, the
Senior College composed of the upper two undergraduate classes
had originally been called the University College to indicate where
true university work began. Other universities might use other
terms, but the way was prepared for the idea that college and graduate study might merge where courses were equally appropriate
and useful for both the advanced undergraduates and the less-ad-
vanced graduate students. Heavy reliance upon such courses would
presently be viewed by some observers as the corruption of the
graduate school and by others as the subversion of liberal education; the fact was that the college was responding to the same ideas
that inspired the founders of the Ph.D. degree and that the college
did so partly on the urging of professors who had attended graduate
school and had come away with a conception of themselves as
professional academics. Bernard Berelson (1960, pp. 20–21) has
effectively disposed of the impression that in 1906 the Carnegie
Foundation worked a revolution in college appointments (and
created the college market for Ph.D. degree holders) by defining
what a college was—for purposes of pension and grant programs—
in terms of graduate work done and Ph.D. degrees taken by faculty
members. At most, the Foundation accelerated tendencies that
had begun years before its own creation. Instruction by professors
bred in the graduate schools had already had its own particular
impact. The sins of the Ph.D. who shirks teaching are so much
with us today that we easily forget that instruction by young scholars and scientists from the American graduate schools—or German
faculties of philosophy—could be a breath of fresh air for undergraduates in the last quarter of the nineteenth century. We know
too little of the colleges from the point of view of the students;
nevertheless, it is plain enough, for example, that before John W.
Burgess went as a young professor from Amherst to Columbia—
to become a founder of graduate studies there—he brought the
intellectual excitement of a new kind of learning to the undergraduates of the college. The case is the more impressive because Am-

herst, thanks to great undergraduate teaching, was by no means a pedagogical desert. John Barnard (1969, pp. 40, 63, 101–102) has discovered that as early as the seventies, the student press at Oberlin was becoming discontented with the intellectual superficiality of instruction and prescribed the appointment of professors with advanced training. That demand would presently be met in part when such young scholars as John R. Commons began to teach at Oberlin. Commons was an alumnus who had, with his friends, organized the Oberlin Henry George Club as a student and had gone on to the Johns Hopkins to rethink his social principles under the inspiration of Richard T. Ely. The pattern of student restiveness and the search for a new education has its obvious modern counterpart, but with a difference. Graduate study was conceived of as a vehicle of academic reform, in the interest of what today would be called intellectual relevance. (See also Rudolph, 1962, pp. 394 ff.; Burgess, 1966, pp. 140–143.)

Within the graduate school, the Ph.D. degree enjoyed prestige, but it was not the only degree offered. It is suggestive that, although the master's degree is much the older degree in the United States, difficulty in defining that degree has been perennial since institution of the Ph.D. degree. The relation of the two degrees has been constantly at issue, and the issue has not been whether the doctorate is a master's plus something added but whether the master's is simply something less than a Ph.D. — a fetal doctorate. In theory, it should be possible to stabilize the meaning of the master's on its own terms; in practice, what can only be called the hegemony of the Ph.D. in American thought about graduate education has prevented agreement on the signification of what is often thought of as the lesser, and not just a different, degree. The hegemony of the Ph.D. as a form is indicated by the sentiment in favor of granting the Ph.D. for the highest study in natural science. Traditionally, *philosophia* and *scientia* had broad and largely overlapping meanings, and it would have been difficult to say that either took precedence over the other where completion of the highest program of studies was to be recognized. When the Ph.D. was established, the adjective *scientific* had wider application (as in *scientific method*) than did *philosophical,* and the usage was the opposite of pejorative. The historian trained to be scientific should not, logically, have bridled at being designated a doctor of science. But the denotation of doctor of philosophy mattered less than its connotations. The meaning of the degree had nothing to do with the ordinary sense of words: when the institution of a doctor of science degree was proposed at the University of Chicago in 1895, the university's leading zoologist was second to none in categorical opposition.

THE MEANING OF PH.D.

The idea of the Ph.D. fired the imaginations of academics. What did the degree stand for in the eyes of the Americans who took the degree themselves and sought to make it possible for others to take it? It is often pointed out that the degree was a German import. Doubtless the American degree owed a large debt to the intellectual and academic awakening that was underway in Germany during the eighteenth century and brought fresh vigor to university life in the next century. Yet as a gloss on the meaning of the American degree, reference to its origins leaves much out. The kinds of study associated with the degree in Germany itself changed over the years, notably as tension between what were later to be called the two cultures increased; and the educational systems and societies that provided the settings of the German and the American Ph.D. degrees differed greatly (Lilge, 1948; Hawkins, 1960, pp. 293–315; Veysey, 1965, pp. 127–138).

There is a clue to the meaning of the degree in the reason that the University of Chicago zoologist, C. O. Whitman, gave for opposing the institution of the doctor of science degree. Differentiation of degrees, he argued, was based upon the idea that the doctorate was given for a *kind* of work done (i.e., its subject) rather than for its *quality.* The emphasis is Whitman's, who said: "To me, the degree of Ph.D. means a mark of scholarship and ability to do ORIGINAL work of a *scientific* order in any line whatsoever. So far as I know, this is the general view" (Storr, 1966, p. 157). Whitman's fellow faculty member, Ernest D. Burton of New Testament studies, summed up a cognate idea: "Quantity of work is not the essential thing" (ibid., p. 155). Behind such views one detects a faith in the unity of inquiry. A single activity of mind should be flagged by a single degree. As it was explained at the turn of the century, Ph.D. work can hardly be thought of apart from the idea of research, which was itself viewed as a crusading cause. The truth existed and was accessible to man, but it had to be sought out. The cause resembled religion in zeal and even in terminology. In 1905, the sociologist Albion Small asserted—indeed preached: "The prime duty of everyone connected with our graduate schools is daily to renew the vow of allegiance to research ideals. . . . The first commandment with promise for graduate schools is: Remember the research ideal, to keep it holy!" (ibid., p. 159). Three years later, G. Stanley Hall, president of Clark University, called the researcher the "Knight of the Holy Spirit of truth." He thought a university existed to keep alive "the holy fervor of investigation" (Veysey, 1965, p. 151). The first recognition of a young man's scholarship was, Hall said, a kind of logical and psychic conversion. Indeed may not conversion to research have played much the same part in the experience of young men and women after the rise of the universities that evangelical conversion had played in the lives of college students previously? The emotions of the student could go beyond professional ambition or dedication to learning for its own sake to become agony over the human condition. John W. Burgess recalled that his career as a political scientist, historian, and graduate dean had its origin in an experience that he had while serving as a sentinel at night on a battlefield of the Civil War. "Is it not possible," he thought, "for man, a being of reason, created in the image of God, to solve the problems of his existence by the power of reason and without recourse to the destructive means of physical violence?" (Burgess, 1966, p. 29). His answer was to devote himself to teaching men how to live by reason and compromise. His language is a reminder that teaching and the inquiry fostered in the graduate school were meant to fuse.[3]

It is an old story that need not be repeated at length—Whitman's testimony has already been given—that the idea of research implied the methods of science. Experimentation was in the ascendent, and the laboratory was the model for places of inquiry, the seminar being explained by likening it to the laboratory. A profound transformation was occurring in the life of the mind as new ways of discovering reality were being tried; a whole school, for John Dewey, or a whole city, for the sociologists, could appear to be a laboratory, too. Supernaturalism, teleological reasoning, and argument from authority were being eclipsed by induction from carefully observed phenomena or from the tested data supplied by critical reading of documents. Such a devoutly religious man as William R. Harper could argue that God's will must be clarified through a process beginning with the authentication of facts derived from the text of the Old Testament, which was to be examined as a record set down by mortal men caught up in human history. Inductive was perhaps Harper's favorite word. One corollary of the scientific method was

[3] For further discussion of this topic, see Church, 1965, pp. 5–10.

the researcher's right to freedom in his pursuit of truth, and another corollary was his obligation to be impartial. Harper's colleague, the geologist T. C. Chamberlin, wrote:

The supreme endeavor is to present a disposition of fairness and openness to all evidence and inductions. Whatever evidence demands, that it accepts. Whichever way the balance of evidence inclines, to that it leans. There is no resistance to the leading of evidence, there is no pressing of evidence to give it greater or less than its intrinsic weight. All lines of inquiry are pursued with equal zest. All phenomena are welcomed with equal cordiality. The mind opens itself on all sides to every avenue of truth with equal impartiality (Storr, 1966, p.161).

A third corollary was specialization of studies. It was not invented in the late nineteenth-century graduate school: the abortive projects of the earlier period had exhibited the pressures building up against general scholarship and the polymath. Both the advancement of research and the development of Ph.D. programs were inextricably connected with the movement towards specialization. It would be a fruitless exercise—the chicken or the egg—to attempt to seek out which was the more significant, that departmentalism fostered specialization in Ph.D. research or that the requirements of such research put a premium on departmental organization. Although the degree might stand for a quality rather than a kind of work, the individual researcher obviously had to concentrate upon something in particular, and the structure of the university reflected that need. Behind the individual department there stood the discipline, of which the department was the local branch. The disciplines multiplied as, for instance, sociology and anthropology split apart; and each acquired a literature, a set of problems, sometimes a distinctive method, and a vocabulary—in sum, a culture of its own. The discipline acquired quasi-judicial significance: a professor under attack because of his ideas could appeal to colleagues in his discipline for certification that his work met their standards. It was in this era that specialists in the same discipline formed themselves into a national association and that the association became the meeting place of professors: American Chemical Society, 1876; Modern Language Association of America, 1883; American Historical Association, 1884; and so on, as each of the specialized disciplines achieved a degree of vertical integration (Berelson, 1960, pp. 14–15). Robert L. Church (1965, pp. 2–3) has concluded that "by the close of the nineteenth century, most social scientists had found that an investigation of the facts was just that and no more, that pure empiricism did not lead to meaningful generalizations." Yet it would be a mistake to think that it was the intention of specialized researchers to learn more and more about less and less. Many European and American social scientists, Church remarks, sought at the outset for an all-embracing truth that was supposed to lie within reality itself.

Describing his seminar, one of those social scientists, the historian Herbert Baxter Adams (1887, p. 168) wrote: "Scattered facts are to be brought together, conflicting evidence is to be sifted down to a residuum of truth, and results are to be reported in the seminary and freshly combined in a scholarly monograph, which shall be a real contribution to science." It was truth that the graduate student was to seek, and it was science, in the singular, that was to be served. The passage is saturated with the thought of the time, not least in the stipulation that the student should make that real contribution and in the implication that it would be published.

Such ideas as Adams voiced can be arranged into a neat set of interlocking concepts and injunctions defining a type of inquiry. Adams nearly did it: facts exist independent of thinking, so begin the process of inquiry by collecting and assaying them like material objects to provide yourself with evidence; evidence reveals truth, so transcribe the truth you observe; your results are a contribution to knowledge—publish! Then you will have earned your doctorate. It is not difficult to piece this formula together from the writings of the time, nor is it difficult to spot where such a scheme, if applied, would invite abuse, e.g., an obsession with factuality, indifference to general ideas, and the fetish of publish-no-matter-what. But such simplistic positivism is a humpty-dumpty that fails to explain either what the Ph.D. represented in the thought of academics when the degree was instituted or why it gained prestige. The ideas associated with the Ph.D. must be set into historical relief, notably against the shadows cast by other ideas to which the advocates of the Ph.D. reacted. We doubt that anybody can find evidence with intrinsic weight as Chamberlin believed; however, he was speaking within living memory of the time when God's purpose at the creation was read teleologically into geology. Examine rocks, he was saying, for signs of concrete natural processes, not proofs of divinity: look for evidence, not evidences. We question the possibility of objectivity if that means that the researcher has not even a hunch in mind when he approaches Adams's "scattered facts"; however, when the social scientists of his generation emphasized the importance of careful fact-gathering, they were thinking of a world that had far less information about itself and its history than we take for granted. Adams did not oppose generalization and indeed had a favorite theory in regard to the origins of American democracy. Also, at least some scholars and scientists were in rebellion against the excogitation of systems in which facts played an illustrative rather than an evidential role: the so-called historical school of economics were asking the now seemingly self-evident question, how do economic institutions actually work? The inductive method as a mode of learning stood in opposition to teaching by precept and the presumption that truth was already known. *Scientific* took some of its meaning from the particular process of experimentation in a laboratory, but it also connoted rigorous criticism in general. Easy acceptance of orthodox views had to be challenged: hence, the painstaking criticism of canonical writings. We may doubt that by adding monograph to monograph, like laying brick on brick to make a tower, one can raise the mind up into sight of Truth, but it is still true that the scholar has a sense of finding truth in a point of textual clarification, if that discovery, with other studies, makes it possible to read a great book, clean and whole. We may reject thoroughgoing departmentalization of learning in favor of interdisciplinary studies; but a century ago, the desideratum in many fields of intellectual endeavor was to provide for such concentration of attention as makes discipline, not to speak of *a* discipline, possible; and the relations between fields were not ignored. The seminar that Herbert Baxter Adams described might well be construed as interdisciplinary today, for it spoke to the interests of men who entered political science, economics, and sociology, as well as history. As to publication: The printed dissertation was not a by-product of education, to justify a special reward if the merits of a particular work warranted its being put into type. To publish was the culmination of the whole process for which the Ph.D. stood: The truth must not only be discovered but also be made known. In that sense, the Ph.D. had deeply social implications; if the idea of research was a quasi religion of the evangelical kind, was it sufficient for good news in the cause of truth to remain on a seminar table? The presumption was that the Ph.D. would have something original to say and hence that had to be said.

The span of mind represented by degree holders was wide. Consider the lives of three Ph.D.'s who were almost of the same age, two having been born in 1856 and the other in 1857, and who reached manhood as the Ph.D. was coming into the ascendant. As a scholar, William R. Harper was nearly the type specimen of the new academic man. After taking his degree in linguistics at Yale in 1875, he never stopped laboring, as an investigator as well as a teacher, for the advancement of a discipline, Hebraic studies. He remained something less than reconciled to the administrative demands he faced as president of the University of Chicago, although he met them with gusto; and he sought always to be a productive scholar—as the phrase is used today. Shortly before his death, he published what he thought of as the crown of his career, commentaries on Amos and Hosea, carrying all the ballast of the footnotes that critics of the Ph.D. like to deride. The signs of original work of a scientific order are all there, but Harper shared a purpose thousands of years old. He sought to discover the will of God in holy texts that souls might be saved. Positivism had no place in his thoughts, but the kind of research associated with the Ph.D. was the pivot of his intellectual life. The case of Woodrow Wilson differs. As a student at the Johns Hopkins University, Wilson had little taste for the "tedious toil of what is known as 'research,'" and he decided against trying for what he called the Ph.D. label. "I have a passion," he confided, "for interpreting great thoughts to the world; I should be complete if I could inspire a great movement of opinion. . ." (Bragdon, 1967, p. 117). The intention was not so different from Harper's fundamental purpose; but it might be supposed that Wilson, who stuck to his opinion about minute research, would have been allowed to drift away from a university that meant Ph.D., with no love lost on either side. In fact, he changed his mind about taking a Ph.D. and was awarded the degree, with a special waiver of final examination, for *Congressional Government.* Wilson's decision did not mark a conversion to "scientific" scholarship, which in his opinion regarded man as subject to, rather than as a source of, power, but Wilson's avowed intentions fit a pattern. "I am," he wrote in his book-cum-thesis, "pointing out facts,—diagnosing, not prescribing remedies," and his ultimate plea was for fearless criticism. When the American system of government had been examined in all its parts without sentiment and by the standards of common sense, it would remain "only to act intelligently upon what our opened eyes have seen. . ." (Wilson, 1956, pp. 205, 215). The pattern of the Ph.D. had to do with just such an opening of eyes. The Johns Hopkins on its side invited Wilson to offer courses as an outside lecturer, and he returned annually for many years. In 1902, he was asked to succeed Herbert Baxter Adams as head of the historical seminar. It was at Princeton, however, that Wilson threw himself into the cause—and the controversy—of a graduate school. The academy did allow Thorstein Veblen to drift away. Like Wilson, Veblen studied at the Johns Hopkins University, but he transferred to Yale and, like Harper, took his Ph.D. there. Arriving at the University of Chicago shortly after its founding, he was befriended by an archpriest of the academy and of conservatism, Professor J. Laurence Laughlin. By the timetable of today, the pace of Veblen's career was slow, but he had company, and when he left the university after more than a decade—perhaps under pressure but without many regrets of his own—the reasons for his departure left his standing as Doctor Veblen unimpaired. Academically, his career had not been very unconventional, but nobody would have called the man, his work, and intellectual style ordinary. It was at Chicago that he wrote the first draft of *The Higher Learning in America*. As published in 1918, the book contained thinly veiled but corrosive portraits of Harper and David Starr Jordan, president of Stanford, where Veblen went after leaving Chicago, and as a whole Veblen's argument can seem, on first reading, a blanket indictment of the university as well as of its builders. But the investigator—the craftsman of scholarship—stands at the center of the picture that Veblen draws of the uncorrupted university, the standard by which Harper and Jordan were found wanting. Indeed much of the sinning of the university builders lay precisely in the fact that they had promoted undergraduate education and university extension, which compromised the role of the investigator. Thus Veblen stood squarely in the tradition of the vertical university—a tradition that had prepared the way for the Ph.D. as the model of the American academic. Admittedly, all three men were exceptional, but the experience of the scholar, the statesman, and the intellectual indicate how flexible the meaning of the Ph.D. could be as it impinged upon human lives.[4]

Finally, the doctorate in the era of its establishment is illuminated indirectly by the criticism it received. It has been noticed more than once that time appears to stand still when the Ph.D. is discussed: what was said a half-century or more ago could, even in rhetoric, be the voices in the faculty club or student commons today (Reed,

[4] For further discussion of Harper's career, see Storr, 1966; of Wilson's academic career, Bragdon, 1967; of Veblen's career, Dorfman, 1961.

1950). The degree is but a little older than a tradition of reaction against it. It was not the beginning of criticism when, in 1903, William James expressed his contempt for the mentality that made the "Ph.D. Octopus" possible. The degree has long had the capacity to make outspoken enemies, but it has also been one of its characteristics that it has inspired its friends, including many in positions of authority, to speak out astringently as well. Dean Andrew F. West of Princeton in 1905 (AAU, 1905, p. 67):

The impulse to produce, produce, produce—a splendid thing when a man cannot help doing a great thing—is an awful thing when second- and third-rate men are being told to produce what they can produce—that is, merely second- and third-rate stuff.

West again in 1908 (ibid., 1908, p. 49):

It [the doctor's dissertation] too often exhibits merely the patiently wrought results of a large quantity of mediocre work. . . . It is too often written under the spur of seeking to find something original. This is apt to result in finding something either unimportant or fictitious. . . . Too many theses exhibit merely or mainly power to arrange, classify, and tabulate; too few dissertations show the power to discover, appropriate, and use only what is valuable, and to develop a given subject analytically and constructively. . . . In conclusion, I feel that the question of the Doctor's dissertation is a question of quality—the quality of a man's general liberal education—the quality of his subsequent graduate work, and above all his own personal quality as a man of bright, deep, sensible, definite intellectual character.

Dean Woodbridge of Columbia in 1912 (ibid., 1912, p. 20):

The [Ph.D.] degree in theory is more representative of certain traditional university ideas than it is of the society which supports our universities or of the students who seek instruction under our graduate faculties or of the educational status of the different departments of knowledge. It stands more for an ideal imposed upon our culture than for an ideal growing out of our culture. . . . The degree aims at being the badge of the proved investigator; the situation makes it an indication of competency to perform certain services. They [degree candidates] come with no uniform preparation, with no common fund of ideas, with few rationalized views of life. They create no common intellectual atmosphere of study and inquiry. Their studies tend to increase their intellectual isolation. They are ready to work, energetic, and ambitious, but they are not rationally disciplined. . . . They graduate, not as accomplished scholars, but as students who by their research have demonstrated their capacity. We are confident of them and hopeful, ready to commend them staunchly. They are, however, prisoners of hope, not sons of Greece.

In the aftermath of the era when the degree was established, its original meaning was perhaps beginning to seem such a prisoner, too.

5. After the Golden Age

Looking backward from the present, we cannot escape seeing a historical paradox: The American graduate schools have collectively realized much that the ideal of the Great American University demanded a century ago—and that then seemed remote from reality indeed—and yet graduate education is implicated, as a principal, in a crisis arising from the most bitter disenchantment with higher education. A dream has come true, but in the eyes of many Americans, it has turned out to be a nightmare. In light of the criticism that graduate education received from its friends, it is possible to say that the graduate school of the Golden Age contained the seeds of paradox, but the present crisis patently owes much to events that occurred after the founders of the American Ph.D. had retired and after that degree had been established—to borrow a term from Thomas S. Kuhn—as the paradigm of graduate education. The emergence of the university characterized by the graduate school can easily be described as a revolution, and its implications had to be spelled out as the twentieth century advanced; but even before the First World War began, the day was past when American graduate education was a novelty. As students, the academics who would shape the university after the war might choose to enroll in the Wilhelmian universities of Germany, but in many fields they could also take for granted the opportunity to have a wholly American education. When a postwar boom started to gain momentum, another era in the history of graduate education was already perhaps a decade old. It had taken the half-century from roughly 1860 to 1910 to establish a practicable mode of graduate education and to cast up its first accounts. For a long time afterward, the paradigm was widely accepted as the guide to normal practice, sometimes as if that was what graduate education simply was. Yet criticism never ceased. Is the era that began before the First World War now coming to an end? Indeed, will it presently seem in retrospect that the era lasted almost exactly another 50 years and that a new era opened in the decade of the sixties? When in 1969 Christopher Jencks and David Riesman wrote the preface to the second edition of *The Academic Revolution,* they felt obliged to explain that the title did not refer to the turmoil of the decade, but is the fact that there was ample reason for misunderstanding their intention an indication that the name of the book was timely? Such questions are somewhat less insistent than they were even so short a time ago as 1969, but they still pose an option. As we look forward, are we to suppose that our fundamental task still is to cope with the aftermath of a cause that began to bear fruit more than a century ago at Yale? Or are we to attempt innovation no less revolutionary than the achievement of the first Golden Age? That puts the option baldly: What happened after 1910, as well as what had happened earlier, suggests the nuances that may be read into that choice (Jencks and Riesman, 1969, p. viii).

A few facts about the period after 1910 are worth rehearsing, although some are familiar. In 1960 Bernard Berelson surveyed much of the ground in *Graduate Education in the United States.* Perhaps the most conspicuous fact is the growth of graduate education—with other parts of education—in sheer size and out of proportion to the growth of the age group most directly involved. Berelson notices that it did not even double between 1900 and 1940, but in his words, "institutions offering the doctorate more than tripled, college faculties became five times as large, college enrollments six times, baccalaureate degrees seven times, and graduate enrollments and degrees from thirteen to seventeen times" (Berelson, 1960, pp. 24–25). The Great Depression did not force a decline in those graduate enrollments, and the boom following World War II must be thought of as the acceleration—admittedly dramatic—of an upward movement already established. In 1961, the centenary year of the American Ph.D., many more than 300,000 students were enrolled in a graduate school of some kind, and about 10,000 received a doctorate (USOE, 1966, Table 1). According to National Research Council records, almost 30,000 doctorates were awarded in 1970—and that number did not include strictly professional degrees. It has been estimated that from 1861 to 1970 inclusive, American universities granted more than a third of a million doctor's degrees, of which half were awarded in the last nine years of the period (Wolfle and Kidd, 1971, p. 784).

Some part of the quantitative growth of graduate education resulted from effort to provide opportunities for graduate study in localities that were not sufficiently well served by the early graduate schools. Although the needs of particular cities had been spoken of when some graduate schools had been established, general demographic requirements had had nothing to do with the selection of their sites. There was no master plan, and hence there was much room for replication, without qualitative change in the original model. Also, the prestige of an individual institution as well as its ability to hold faculty could depend—or seem to depend—upon its building a graduate school according to standard specifications, and a new generation could be inspired by the same ideals that informed the first universities, which indeed perpetuated them. William H. Pyle, a Cornell Ph.D. of 1909 and an advocate of graduate study at Wayne State University at Detroit, spoke in 1938, for example, as the latter-day counterpart of the founding fathers of graduate education: "Graduate work means *advanced* work if it means anything. . . . We split hairs and multiply courses. Graduate courses should deal with fundamentals." And in 1940: "Our community will make a great mistake if it does not make research possible at Wayne State. Our Graduate School should be the instrument of our community for studying the great problems in the fields of education, sociology, economics, and government, that must be solved if civilization is to survive . . ." (Hanawalt, 1968, pp. 303 and 315). Yet the expansion of graduate education, as if to a new order of magnitude, meant something more than, indeed something different from, the fulfillment of the old research-oriented ideals of advanced study. In the opinion of qualified observers, the substance of graduate education changed as its forms were put to vocational uses. In 1932, Dean Howard Lee McBain of Columbia wrote (and the theme was not novel):

We all recognize, I suppose, much as we hate to admit it, that every graduate school in this country is in essence, as far as the major portion of its student body's economic, intellectual, and spiritual outlook is concerned, a teachers college. It is, so to say, an abnormal normal school, refusing to confess or even to face its nature. Whether we like it or not, the Doctor's degree has come to have high commercial value. It is, in consequence, pursued by large numbers who have great interest in the degree but little or no interest in, or capacity for, genuine research. . . . The task is undertaken not for the sake of the subject but for the sake of the degree. Many of these [students] plow and plug and ultimately win the coveted reward. It is their first and, so help them God, their last sally into this stupid business of research (AAU, 1932, p. 71).

That judgment is somewhat a caricature, at any rate if it is applied to the period after World War II. Berelson found that in eight out of nine disciplines the majority of persons who took doctorates in 1947–48 published one or more titles other than the dissertation in less than a decade after receiving the degree (Berelson, 1960, pp. 54–55). It would be difficult to argue, however, that graduate education would have expanded as much as it did if the appeal of research had not been massively reinforced by the premium put upon the possession of advanced degrees in the professions and by the multiplication of the professions themselves. Reciprocal thrusts were working like a jack to push graduate education up as a central girder of American society. The *curriculum vitae* reflected what more and more lives meant. It is exaggeration, but hardly falsification, to say that American opportunity was becoming academicized as, in a demographic shift of revolutionary proportions, youth moved from the family, the fields, and the workshop into formal education—first elementary school, presently high school, next the college, and then the graduate school. In the 1830s, Alexis de Tocqueville could write about democracy in America without giving more than passing attention to formal education, but a century later Dean F. J. E. Woodbridge would notice what he thought was an astonishing dependence on supervised instruction. "Our population is generally school-conscious and school-dependent" (AAU, 1932, p. 107). The graduate school was asked to provide opportunity on those terms, most notably perhaps in the ramifications of the teaching profession.

It was part of Dean McBain's argument in 1932—although tentatively put—that the degree of doctor of education should not be confined to the category of students who specialized in education. In that same year, President Wallace W. Atwood of Clark favored the award of the doctor of arts degree for broad, general, cultural training up to the highest stage. His reasoning gives a clue to what numbers meant. The standard of the Ph.D. had been lowered: "We have no degree now that is exclusively held by men who are devoted to research in various academic fields" (AAU, 1932, p. 58–59). If that was so, the Ph.D. as a form had been emptied of its original meaning.

That is not of course to say that research languished in the American universities. On the contrary, it was in the period between the World Wars that research came into its own. The ideal had been established earlier, but the funding of research had usually been left, as it were, to the regular payroll and to ordinary expenditures for library and laboratory. A professor's salary provided his research grant. Thus, President Harry P. Judson of the University of Chicago would write to President G. Stanley Hall of Clark: "We expect work in research to be done normally by all our staff, and to that end we try not to overburden them with teaching. In some cases we have given special inducements to carry on a particular piece of research, by relieving the officer in question of a part of his normal duties" (Storr, 1954, p. 168). No endowment specifically devoted to the support of research and publication existed, but Judson opened a window toward the future when he advocated the creation of such a fund from gifts. In the twenties and thirties, other universities made similar plans for the funding of research: the University of California anticipated that movement in 1915 by organizing a Board of Research with a budget of $2,000 (Stadtman, 1970, pp. 212–213). The philanthropic foundations brought their larger resources to bear, sometimes as grants or fellowships to individual professors but also in support of projects. The political scientist Charles E. Merriam wrote in 1921: "Science is a great cooperative enterprise in which many intelligences must labor together. There must always be wide scope for the spontaneous and unregimented activity of the individual, but the success of the expedition is conditioned upon some general plan of organization" (Storr, 1954, pp. 173–174). Individualistic investigation, which Judson described with emphatic approval as something wholly personal in character, did continue, despite short rations, but the big campaigns that Merriam envisaged were successfully mounted, notably along interdisciplinary lines. Precedents were at hand during World War II and after when federal agencies began to write contracts for research, and grants became a fact of academic life. Investigation could be supported at levels that would have seemed incredible when the universities first started to seek special funds for research: again a change in orders of magnitude had occurred.

Although from the time when graduate education was founded particular American professors had deserved membership in the international community of scholarship and science (Josiah W. Gibbs being a classic example), it seems accurate to say that American research by and large did not attain full stature internationally until well after the beginning of this century. That achievement is one of the distinguishing marks of the era that followed the original period of university building. Was it a cause or a test of the stature of American research that American universities absorbed leaders of research from Europe when Hitler drove them out? Concurrently, the idea of research began to permeate the culture. Advertising picked up "laboratory testing," and third-grade teachers might assign "research" papers, but obviously something vastly more serious was happening. Research was being thought of as an enterprise in the outcome of which the life and fate of the nation were implicated. Research was becoming a national interest, and the planning of national manpower for research became a topic of high policy. Where else but in the graduate school should such manpower in many fields have its source?

The anomaly of the situation is indicated by the conflict that has long existed over the Ph.D. in relation to college teaching. According to what may be called the purist tradition, the college and the university differ in essence, and if the graduate school as the heart of the university becomes concerned about anything but pure research or research itself as a profession, at best the university will waste its resources and at worst betray its ideals. On the other side, there is the tradition of complaint—which Dean McBain's remarks illustrated—that Ph.D. programs are not designed to prepare the holders of the degree for the profession of teaching that so many of them enter. That view may also be premised upon the difference between college and university, or more exactly, college and graduate school. The view leads to the conclusion, not that research should be preserved from contamination, but rather that liberal education should be saved from seduction—or even rape. In the words of Earl J. McGrath in 1959 (pp. 14–15):

Under the spreading influence of graduate education, the liberal arts colleges shifted their emphasis from teaching to research; from instruction concerned with the key ideas of Western culture to instruction composed of the latest findings in ever narrower areas of scholarly investigation; from a concern with the complete development of mind and character which Milton believed fitted "a man to perform justly, skillfully, and magnanimously all the offices, both private and public, of peace and war" to the cultivation of the professional skills and the restricted subject matter of the various fields of intellectual endeavor—in brief, from the dissemination to the creation of knowledge. To a considerable extent the weaknesses, the ineptitudes, and the inadequacies of higher education today have their origin in these changes. . . .

In 1955, the Committee of Fifteen had proposed a basis for mediation, i.e., that Ph.D. programs should be designed to educate the scholar-teacher, whose ultimate choice between research and teaching would be determined neither by inability to teach nor by incompetence as a creative scholar. The actual presence of such scholar-teachers, as I believe, has steadied the university and its relation to the college over a long period, but the place of research in graduate education and the latter's role in the preparation of teachers remain matters of passionate dispute (Strothmann, 1955, p. 15; see also Perkins and Snell, 1962, pp. 160–187).

What is sometimes overlooked—and it is another mark of the era—is that the college, and thus the preparation of the graduate student, are not what they were when graduate education was founded. At about the time the era began, reform of the college was inspired by ideas that did not have their source or most conspicuous manifestation in American graduate education. In some part because of the return of the first Rhodes scholars, British models again became influential; indeed, partly because of freshened energy in the tradition of the liberal culture, specialization was made to give some way to general education—and not always against the will of academics deeply committed to the ideal of research. The ideal itself implied a demand for minds sufficiently broad to ask the right questions, and professors and administrators responsible for graduate education said so. Needless to say, the impact of collegiate reform was fluctuating and uneven, but the intellectually ambitious student did not have to live in *purdah:* it should be remembered that even the original Stover approached graduation with the uneasy sense that he had missed something. The case of the independent colleges is especially revealing. At the turn of the century, it could be seriously asked whether a college without a graduate school, the "small college," was a vestigial institution without a future, but at mid-century, it became clear that such colleges were a prime source of scholarly and scientific talent. Many invigorated colleges, whether independent or belonging to universities, created yet more pressure upon graduate studies by introducing undergraduates to the excitement of intellectual life. On graduation day, theirs was the hunger of people who know what eating well can be (Thomas, 1962).

During the transformation of higher education in the nineteenth century, it was the college that was the recipient of new, stimulating intellectual forces. In our day, it cannot be said that the tables are turned, because the graduate schools remain powerful generators, but the best of the undergraduates are encouraged by the best of the college professors to ask questions that are more highly charged intellectually than many thesis topics. Perhaps there is much that is shallow in general education and much that is impracticable in the projects of undergraduates; it can hardly be doubted that the first year of graduate school often provides a necessarily astringent emphasis upon method. But undergraduate inquiry versus graduate discipline is a false dichotomy. When graduate study was first proposed, it did make sense to insist upon the difference between collegiate drill in the established rudiments of general learning and the free pursuit, in the university, of new, specialized knowledge. Although that separation of purposes probably did scant justice to some undergraduate instruction and more than justice to what might actually happen in a university, the argument was not wildly unrealistic. The college curriculum was a closed box upon which another box, open at the top, was to be placed. But that metaphor became obsolete as the new knowledge was introduced into the college curriculum, bringing both specialization as to subject matter and the idea of critical inquiry as to method. A more realistic figure today is two upright, somewhat overlapping wedges placed butt to edge. The wedge standing butt-down represents the more general part of the student's higher education, tapering off toward the top; the other wedge is specialized education, occupying more and more space toward its upper end. The figure suggests the argument that the wedges should be exactly side by side so that the student is not without some specialized study at the beginning of higher education and is still engaged explicitly with general questions at its end. The problem before the graduate school is whether, and if so how, it should exploit the cognate facts that the intellectual life of students may well begin long before entry into graduate school and that the particular kind of intellectual activity to which many students are already habituated is neither wholly specialized nor wholly general. The increasing concentration of the student's thinking in the latter years of college may not only crystallize plans for a career but also give added momentum to general inquiry. Despite the growth of professionalism, the questions with which the student feels impelled to come to terms may not be professional; insofar as graduate education is in fact organized around questions of the professional kind, it will will give an answer to the student's query only as a by-product of study, if at all.

What does the graduate school offer the student? We do not have to wait for the writing of a full-scale history of graduate study during the past half-century to know that within a static form, the substance has exploded. In catalogs of graduate schools, the general regulations may be a set piece, but the sections on the several departments and interdisciplinary programs have become so fat that the binding gives way in the hand. The thickness of catalogs is but the most obvious mechanical evidence of the variety of enterprises that flourish under the rubric of the doctorate, and the offerings of the masters' curricula extend the list. Graduate study has been indeed fecund.

LOOKING AHEAD: THE NATURE OF OUR CHOICES Some observers suspect that the proliferation of programs has passed the point of diminishing returns and that they are not all worth the effort. It can hardly be doubted that some instruction makes a mockery of education by stultifying thought: what sometimes passes as practice in research works less like a sharpening grindstone than a pulverizing millstone. As we turn our minds toward the future, however, it would be foolish to begin making plans by simply writing off the past. The issue must not be reduced to a simple choice between conservatism and radicalism. Undoubtedly, there is a tendency to debate higher education in terms of confrontation. Discussion has become polarized around such issues as the classics versus science, the lecture versus the seminar, or general versus specialized education. Controversy between adversaries inspires belief that only a fight to the finish can decide which way the university will move, not infrequently as if toward the millennium. For higher education has, like religion, been deeply colored by chiliasm. That kind of response to crisis has the virtue of bringing false consensus to light, and it certainly has lent emotional force to the attack upon business-as-usual. In the realm of graduate studies, putative dichotomies are at hand. College versus graduate school, human relevance versus professionalism, and teaching versus research have already become set pieces; and academics are even now standing up to be counted. The response, however, has its price, and it's too high. Terms must be oversimplified and reality distorted, with the result that the response is ultimately self-defeating. *Procrustean* was a favorite adjective among critics of the old-fashioned college, and it is the right word for the process of forcing debate about graduate education into unmodified either/or terms. What is lopped off a complex issue to make a pat case today is enough to create another crisis tomorrow. It settled nothing a century and a half ago to choose up sides for a fight between the classics and science because the formulation was artificial. Although that controversy produced a seesaw effect that might be mistaken for a dialectical movement toward a higher order of education, the true dialecticians were not the polemicists but rather those humanists and scientists who refused to opt for the simple dichotomy and instead brought critical inquiry to bear upon both man and nature.

The obvious defects of graduate study make it too easy to forget the intellectual vitality that the best in graduate study has fostered: criticism of the worst is in danger of becoming more a ritual of exorcism than a starting point of change. It is sufficient answer to any blanket charge against graduate education that first-rate senior professors do find junior colleagues of like quality to welcome each year; the stream never dries up. There is a striking discrepancy between general criticism and the enthusiasm that specific students inspire. It is a mystery well worth exploring that the graduate school seldom gives official recognition, as the college frequently does, to a difference between ordinary and honors degrees, but that letters of recommendation do unofficially confer the Ph.D. with honors: there are the often indistinguishable sketches of the industrious young doctors who have written good, solid dissertations; and there is the glowing portrait of the particular mind that your department really cannot afford to ignore. However informally, the high quality of some Ph.D.'s is acknowledged and indeed honored.

The fact has significance in regard to reform. It has been argued that requirements for the doctorate have successfully resisted change because the custodians of the Ph.D. have had both a vested interest in the degree and the power to put down its rivals. Yet the possibility remains that the form has resisted change, in some important part, precisely because a long line of Ph.D.'s—although not the whole body of them—have by their actual performance justified the identification of the degree with truly original research. When Albion Small said, "Remember the research ideal, to keep it holy!" he understood that a graduate school might produce countless mediocrities, but he believed that more glory lay "in stimulating one mind to a genuinely critical attitude towards conventional ideas." The fact that such glory has been achieved more than once may help to explain why the form of the Ph.D. has itself become a sanctified convention and why the recognition of special honors is left to unofficial expressions of judgment. If the attitude Small had in mind is—like virginity—absolute, its emblem hardly admits of shadings (Storr, 1966, p. 159).

But it is one thing to prove that the high claims of the Ph.D. are sometimes made good and another thing altogether to argue that contentment over the state of graduate education is justified. France in the eighteenth century and Russia in the nineteenth produced brilliant men. I take it for granted that a crisis exists and submit that the reasons for its existence indeed have fully as much to do with the fact that the successes of the Ph.D. have given that degree a sustained attractiveness as with the other, notorious fact that stupid crimes against education have been committed in its name. However entrenched its supporters may be, it is difficult to imagine that a revolt against its hegemony would not have been victorious long since if the defects of the Ph.D. were not those of a virtue that is tacitly acknowledged. The critically important task is not to destroy a monopoly held by an arbitrary exercise of power, which would make the task wholly political, but rather to ensure that the influence of the Ph.D. or any other degree, however worthy in itself, does not make a balanced response to the just claims upon the graduate school impossible. That task reaches far beyond academic politics because it entails the essentially intellectual process of defining what the several degrees should be, both in relation to each other and in relation to culture and society.

But there is the logically prior question of whether the provision of degree programs exhausts the responsibility of the graduate school. For a century or so, history has been preparing us to take it for granted that graduate education is composed, as if by natural law, of molecules called degree programs. Studies are customarily altered by adding or subtracting courses, which play the part of atoms in the system, or by otherwise changing the set of requirements that give form to each program. Because this mode of thought was established as part and parcel of graduate education when such education was itself established, it is easy to suppose that graduate education and study toward degrees are identical. The supposition is reinforced by the obvious connection between the proliferation of degree programs and the growth of the population of graduate students. The ever increasing variations on the theme of the degree program, especially at the level of the master's degree, has demonstrated no less how adaptable a device the degree program is than how ready the graduate school is to try variations. Yet it does not necessarily follow that the sufficiency of the device is, if anything, more than amply proven; a century of experience has made resort to programming habitual and attention to it obsessive. It is not self-evident that graduate study and its standards would fall into ruin if degree programs were dismantled, simply leaving acknowledged masters of research and teaching to certify what the students are individually prepared to do, and how well.

The term *graduate education* obscures a distinction between the approaches we may take to defining what education beyond college may mean to the student. Do we begin by considering what the college has already enabled the student to learn, or by determining what the advanced degree should stand for when the student ultimately wins it? On the one hand, there is that education that is defined—in a sense, negatively—by the discrepancy between what the college offers and what there is to learn. That education is postbaccalaureate: on commencement day, the graduate is likely to want more knowledge and to need more if the accumulating resources of learning and science are to be brought to bear fully on the problems that the graduate faces in a calling or as a human being. In the language of one slogan, that kind of education is truly lifelong learning. Part of it means going to the library to keep up with the literature of a topic, whether out of duty or as a hobby; and another part consists of picking up more or less elementary knowledge that one did not elect to study in college and nobody would expect the graduate school to offer. A third part, however, is the pursuit of knowledge in those fields or "majors" with which one did become familiar before leaving college but in which face-to-face instruction is still a great benefit or even a necessity. In the arts and science, the graduate school is the most appropriate institution for such study, but not necessarily with regard to the earning of degrees as such. On the other hand, there is the education that is defined positively by the fact that requirements are laid down: before taking the degree, the candidate (which the graduate becomes) shall demonstrate a reading knowledge of French or German, pass examinations in so many courses or fields, write an acceptable thesis, etc., according to the design of the particular program. Such education is less accurately described as postbaccalaureate than as premagisterial or predoctoral. As its terms may or may not coincide with the student's hopes and felt needs on college graduation day, the question is whether the graduate school should accept responsibility for graduate education under the terms of but one or of both of the definitions.

Consider a connotation of the word *university* (that, incidentally, used to be cited to give the word a false etymology)—the idea of the university as a repository of universal knowledge. A century and more ago, the advocates of what we now call graduate study did speak of degree requirements from time to time, but they found it entirely possible to focus their attention as much upon what the student ought to have as upon what the student ought to do. Going to college was not enough; Americans should have access to the riches of learning and science that lay beyond the undergraduate curriculum. That was the essential argument, and it was the mission of the university, as distinct from the college, to open the door of the treasury. Perhaps it was partly because the pioneers of reform were acutely anxious over the relative poverty in which American higher education existed that they used a rhetoric that now seems romantically inflated: the restraint of the Virginia commissioners, who were careful to say that they were talking about an indefinite and not an infinite expansion of knowledge, is a refreshing relief. Yet the vision of opulence in learning and science did fire the imaginations of academics; and they talked of the open university. Today, massive resources of learning and science are at hand. Academics continue to experiment with ways to open up the university, but the end of deprivation has made it easy to adopt the convenient, even complacent, view that the mounting of successful degree programs entirely satisfies those claims upon the graduate school that are derived from the idea of the university as a repository. Yet it must not be forgotten that, despite the learning that is now available in college courses, the situation of the student has not altogether changed during the past century; of course, what there is to learn has expanded enormously. The graduate can still ask: Where can I find the knowledge that will satisfy my intellectual need? Suppose that we do opt for the idea of university as repository: statistically, the number of students who are not at least moderately happy to be working toward fulfillment of requirements may be insignificant, but the presence of the ninety-and-nine who are seeking a degree fails, in principle, to outweigh the obligation of the graduate school to provide wholeheartedly for the other student who just wants to learn.

More and more students appear to have little or no interest in taking degrees except as a need to meet job specifications imposes an interest in the crassest meaning of the word. But what is at issue is less whether the graduate school should provide for two wholly different populations of students than to what extent the graduate school should take explicit account, institutionally, of what used to be called the love of learning—whether or not it be the sole reason that the individual student has for remaining in the university. Is there any doubt that innumerable students are seeking knowledge for its own sake as well as for the prestige or professional standing that a degree confers? The span of intentions from pure truth seeking to mere careerism obviously has a wide middle-section of laminated motives. Undoubtedly, too, as a result of becoming lively communities intellectually and culturally—rallying points as often as degree mills—the universities have informally provided graduate students a kind of further education that they want and that no curriculum describes. What the student argues about regularly at lunch, and with whom, determines much of the meaning that going-to-graduate-school has. In addition, can it be questioned that what typically enlivens teaching for the professor and makes the profession a source of delight is discovery of the student who is not content simply to touch all the bases that the rules specify? The fact is sometimes overlooked that semantically the reality of graduate work at its best is paradoxical: where the professor and student so truly join forces intellectually that degree requirements cease to govern the relationship, work becomes a kind of play and, in the strict sense of the term, a part of the extracurriculum. In the light of what academics, both students and professors, actually do at a good university, it may be argued that degree programs resemble but the facade of a treasure house. Yet the double question remains: Does the masonry of that facade sometimes extend back so far as to constitute rigidly designed corridors, and are the doors themselves still too narrow—which is very different from asking if the thresholds are too high.

The university as a repository cannot be distinguished from the university as a place where students learn how to seek out and organize knowledge for themselves. In that connection, does it suffice for the university, or more particularly the graduate school, to offer degree programs that familiarize the student with research? In the broadest usage, *research* covers everything from mere compilation of facts according to some formula—or even looking a topic up in the *Encyclopedia Britannica*—to seminal work by the best minds; but usage so inflated is no help. Even in application to Ph.D. dissertations *research* is an omnibus word embracing different kinds of activity; the operations that a mathematician or a theoretical physicist performs are not identical with the explication of texts for which a Ph.D. in English may be awarded, whereas the experimenter in science and the humanistic historian have tasks that are distinct from each other and from the others as well. Requirements often tilt toward empirical research, but perhaps just as often what marks the dissertation deemed best is the author's capacity for modes of thought—e.g., conceptualization —which are not themselves the particular mark of such research. On the face of the evidence, the meaning of the word as applied to Ph.D. work is in a state of some disarray. There may be a least common denominator, that research is the discovery of new ideas or facts that illuminate knowledge—and at its best that activity is beyond price—but it has long been a standing charge against research done for the dissertation that too often the addition it makes to knowledge is too trivial to justify the pain. If contributing to knowledge is what is required, such results give *contribution* a core of meaning too insignificant to govern any program worthy of a university (CGS, 1970, p. 71 ff.).

It is useful to turn the whole matter of definition around and to ask not what particular activities customarily find a place under the rubric of research, but what meaning we wish to assign it in reference to inquiry in general. The two words *inquiry* and *research* are sometimes employed as synonyms, but suppose that they are thought of separately. Inquiry can be seen in the largest sense as the aggregate of man's efforts to rescue whatever is in his ken from absurdity, with *research* reserved to designate some concrete process or congeries of such processes by which inquiry is carried out. Inquiry is enormously complex, indeed paradoxical. Donald Fleming (Fleming and Bailyn, 1969, p. 165) has written of Niels Bohr's thought in regard to the principle of complementarity: "The object now became to discover the most fundamental, because mutually exclusive, alternatives for describing nature [not to mention man and society] and then to integrate these within the paradox that each was required to eke out the deficiencies of the other." Inquiry is an aspect of universal history and of prehistory as well, and it must be thought of as still evolving. Perhaps it should be considered less as a distinct activity in itself than as a mutable exponent of human existence. Arthur Lovejoy spoke of the great chain of being; in a somewhat similar sense, we can speak of a chain of inquiring, which links minute observation and sweeping generalization. Inquiry, like love, eludes final description. It may be seen as a flowing, unfolding, growing, coruscating response of mind—the metaphors increase—and it is unpredictable. It need not proceed by the solution, in series, of fixed problems; it can begin with nothing more than uneasiness of mind, which acts like a signal bell. There is a discrepancy somewhere between the accepted view of things and what I think I am seeing right now. The mind stirs, and questions begin to multiply, as if spontaneously. Inquiry has indeed been compared to a game, and it offers a fierce joyousness. It has, too, the waywardness caught, as well as demonstrated, by Veblen's defense of idle curiosity. Yet over the centuries, inquiry has plainly been thought of as a source of power, once without a clear distinction being observed between magic and truth. Mystery meant potency, and the "mysteries" of the several callings were valued as secrets. However, the awe a Faust once inspired has given ground, although not entirely, to belief that the sequel to inquiry must be the announcement of its findings to mankind. Today its fate appears to be implicated in understanding what inquiry is.

As the contrast between the scientific and magical interpretation of nature illustrates, inquiry reveals inner tensions. It might be said that given the option of seeking truth in accord with the dictates of superstition or science, in its most sweeping sense, the university had to make, and did make, its choice (at least in principle) when its history began, but a variety of approaches to inquiry remained available—and debatable. For generations, scholasticism exerted a powerful influence as a model of inquiry, but the issue of nominalism versus realism did not disappear, and presently the issue of science in something like its modern sense did appear. Again and again, the university has come to a point where it could be supposed that inquiry had become sharply polarized and that a choice of approaches to inquiry had to be made. Should the university stand for but one kind of inquiry, *the* academic mode, whichever it is? We continue to debate the distinction between deductive and inductive reasoning, between empirical or experimental and theoretical work, between the examination of particulars and the pursuit of general laws, between discovering facts and originating concepts, and between analysis and synthesis. In the modern sense of *science,* we also distinguish between scientific and humanistic insight. We detect a difference between the attempt to solve the problems or "puzzles" that are generated by debate back-and-forth within the confines of a single discipline and the attack upon questions that agonize a whole society, and we notice that neither of those approaches to inquiry is identical with the scrutinizing of semantic, logical, or mathematical relationships between terms. What do we expect of inquiry? Is it essentially speculative discourse—or an exchange of concepts or models—about something behind a screen, something by which human thought cannot be tested directly and conclusively, or does inquiry allow and entail an encounter with reality, face to face? Is inquiry always an approach at most, and never arrival? The differences that we see in the conduct of inquiry stem only partly from disagreement over the validity of particular processes of thought; we must cope in the first instance with a disparity among the expectations that determine what we mean by validity and even think about at all. The intellectual attitude of the student is of course influenced by elements of personality and experience that the university cannot pretend to affect, but insofar as the student's attitude is also influenced by instruction, both formal and informal, the university can hope to be effective. So the strategic question: Should the graduate school be founded on the premise that the approaches to inquiry differ so widely on a scale of intrinsic worth, as well as in kind, that a hierarchy of approaches, if not just one, should govern the life of the school? If so, which and in what order? The alternative is to find, pluralistically, that at least some attitudes toward inquiry, if not all, are of equal worth and deserve equal reinforcement. (It may be that the pedagogical situation will warrant heavier emphasis upon a particular approach in formal instruction, on the grounds that the academic community as a whole or society at large will provide students with sufficient incentive and opportunity to become familiar with the others, but that is a matter of tactics.) If the graduate school has an obligation to the cause of inquiry, where does that obligation cease to consist of making choices that result in the subordination or rejection of some tendencies within inquiry and become a duty to encourage students in a sweeping exploration of all the possibilities our curiosity allows?

It hardly needs to be said that the processes of thought demand attention because they are the medium not only of inquiry but also of the education and training designed to advance it. Let it stand without argument that the graduate school has a responsibility, at its level of education, to match each of the university's intentions in regard to inquiry with an opportunity for the student to carry forward an appropriate process of thought. Such matching regularly occurs in practice and is no new departure: a good case can be made that the reason why *research* has a variety of nuances today is that it has become the custom to speak of the process appropriate to every fresh line of inquiry as research. Some academics will contend that the meaning of *research* has been extended so far that sound inquiry as well as the traditional association of the word with closely applied methods of empirical investigation has been put in jeopardy. There is, however, the other question of whether the graduate school has been as aggressive as it might be and as self-aware as it can be in exploring the possibilities of inquiry and establishing its intentions in accord with the findings. What those intentions are must be considered when anybody challenges the soundness of particular processes of thought designed to carry inquiries forward. Has the graduate school exploited its present situation to the optimum advantage of inquiry?

Some clues to what the graduate school might do can be found in the history of recent decades; in fact, signs are all around us. It has been argued that the idea of inquiry held by academics in the Golden Age was not the crabbed thing that a positivistic formula for research suggests; similarly it can be argued that precisely the same multiplicity of meanings that has made *research* in modern usage a loosely defined word should be read as a provocative indication of the capacity for growth that the processes of thought have. The development of new methods has been no less striking than the multiplication of fields and subfields of study. Although some philosophers are convinced that the practitioners in the several disciplines are neither sufficiently self-conscious nor critical enough in regard to methodology, the discussion of procedures continues—thanks partly to a recognized need to define what truly professional methods are. It is merely antiquarian to wonder if the founders of graduate education had any idea of the proliferation of methods that we take for granted, but it would be a mistake of critical importance if we take it too much for granted. Both the wise direction of inquiry, lest the energies available to it be sapped by pretentious novelty, and the wholehearted support of genuine innovation—as well as wise judgment as to which is which—depend upon understanding explicitly what the causes of growth are. Inquiry itself is an expanding topic of study, and not only among the epistemologists. The sociology of knowledge and the psychology of insight are only two of the specialties—in history there are several—that illuminate the nature of inquiry. An increasing body of writing deals with its context, e.g., with the economics of education. The present situation is both expansive and fluid; but does the organization of graduate studies reflect as much as it might the promise that the situation holds? The development of methodology, discipline by discipline, and the further study of inquiry as such have yet to be thought of generally as complementary activities, each of which will be the more fruitful where the results of the other are kept explicitly in mind. Inquiry into the nature of inquiry can of course be maintained as a specialty, but it will not be wholly effective until its findings permeate the culture of the academy. In the light of that possibility, there is the prospect that the development of particular methods and the exploration of inquiry itself will be advanced as parts of a single process. It can be the intention of the graduate school to provide not only that an appropriate method is devised to match each particular line of inquiry that some scholar or scientist may wish to pursue, but also that no approach to inquiry is left untested for want of experimentation with a method. Whether the word *research* is restricted in usage to empirical investigation or is applied broadly to cover any proven mode of thought is an issue that should be settled—but by agreement on definitions. What matters in substance is whether the graduate school should provide the student with a context of life, as well as a degree program, that encourages such inquiry as is both rigorous and free.

Another clue to the possibilities before the graduate school is the growing conviction that the digestion of knowledge has, by and large, not kept pace with the increase in specialized fields. It is not only the layman who wants to know what it all means: indeed, it seems clear enough that if the exploration of vast, underdeveloped sources of information was at the heart of a great cultural movement in the nineteenth century, we are becoming engaged in a comparable great movement to extract meaning from the stores of data now at hand. The construction of retrieval systems and memory banks is but the technical manifestation of a passionately felt need that cannot be met without inquiry of the most far-reaching sort. Such inquiry demands the critical analysis of much larger bodies of literature than the writer of the learned article or monograph is usually obliged to consider directly, and of course, it requires synthesis on the grand scale. The task is awesome, but here and there scholars and scientists have committed themselves to it. In another age, the task would have been called philosophical: Should graduate students—some of whom are candidates for the degree of doctor of philosophy—be admitted to that search? Perhaps the door should be opened only very cautiously lest ill-prepared students flounder on the sill, but is it in the unalterable nature of graduate education that such inquiry cannot proceed as a continuation, without a lapse, of the synthesis begun in college? It does not follow that the direction of the work of the graduate student is merely a prolongation of college training. Unless the college and the graduate school have identical purposes, it is to be expected that graduate study will redirect the flow of the student's thought. Grant that the intellectual purpose of the college, whether its curriculum allows specialization or not, is to enable the mind of the student to find its general bearings: such education entails inquiry, but not necessarily either the full mastery of technique or the pursuit of answers that are new not only to the inquirer but to mankind. It is experience with that kind of inquiry that graduate study should provide the student—as quickly as possible and as fully as the processes of disciplined thought allow.

It is a cognate clue that the integration of knowledge is pursued no less across traditional boundaries than within particular fields. It has long since been the mission of interdisciplinary committees or institutes to foster synthesis by exploring the possibilities for thought at the points where the established disciplines meet. Hyphenated studies now gain recognition as disciplines in themselves; yet in the crass but evocative slang phrase, the place "where the action is" may be without a name of its own for some time. Investigators from different disciplines but with similar questions in mind simply find themselves talking together—perhaps with a sense of discovery and delight. Presently the group may be organized formally and given funds to support its work; ultimately it may be conceived of as a department in itself, where appointments can be made and a distinctive career line established. Some such process, for example, is currently going on where history, sociology, and geography meet, and both computerized analysis and the theory of structures appear likely to produce new configurations of investigation. Such studies may be most stimulating at their beginning, when—in the terms of early Christianity—two or three are gathered together. The graduate student stands somewhere between the saint in search of God's truth and the gambler looking for the action, but the best time for the student to find a calling intellectually, if not professionally, may be the moment when ideas are being first incubated. As long ago as 1896, William R. Harper observed: "The work of the student in the future will not be cut off into departments; on the contrary it will be the study of problems which will lead him into and through many departments of study" (Storr, 1966, p. 94). In our time, such study as Harper anticipated may involve greater risk to departmentalized careers—or at least a far more complex skein of professional considerations—than it did in 1896, and those considerations cannot be ignored. Yet artificial, as distinct from the functional, requirements of academic life must not be allowed to remain standing as obstacles to the student's attack upon such problems as Harper described. The issue is not whether the academic department as an institution is obsolete— it performs extremely valuable services both to persons and disciplines—but rather whether departmentalism as a habit of thought still operates to inhibit the student whose thinking falls outside departmental categories.

The issue of professionalism cannot be left out. It has been claimed time and again that the graduate faculty of the arts and sciences is actually as professional as law or medicine and the other schools that are explicitly so. Certainly the line between the schools is often vague in regard both to the content of studies and to the intentions of the members—not least because "pure" inquiry cannot be defined by institutional boundaries. The British are speaking about the hiving off of certain enterprises that can be separated from nationalized industry; and certainly a hiving off of professional and quasi-professional studies has occurred in the American universities, sometimes within the boundaries of the graduate school itself. The institution of programs for the doctor of arts degree is such an event; and of course the case for the professional character of the graduate school rests partly on the indications—which are neither the whole truth nor a lie—that the establishment of the Ph.D. degree itself depended upon the hiving off of college and university teaching as a profession. A distinction must be drawn between preparing for a chosen calling by studying its particular arts and being found qualified for entry into an occupation after demonstrating that one has been called to seek the truth; however, the issue is not whether a process of professionalization has been going on—it has—but whether it is desirable for some part of the university—presumably the graduate school—to be explicitly charged with responsibility for offering such advanced instruction in the arts and science as students demand for other than professional reasons. In Thorstein Veblen's sense of the term, what play should idle curiosity have?

The question itself is not idle; on the contrary, it raises a profound issue as to the conception we have of the knowledge that falls, at any given moment, outside of a professional context. It is the issue of the academic imagination as it is confronted by the amplitude of learning and science today. One must speak impressionistically, but it seems safe to say that the American university today is richer in knowledge than the university of 1910 by at least as high a ratio as it surpassed the old-fashioned college. In many fields, work done a half-century ago—or perhaps much more recently than that—resembles the primitives of the art world; and the middle-aged professor may well have to reconcile himself to being looked upon as belonging among the ancestors of his discipline. The advancement and refinement of knowledge owes much to the incentives that professionalism has provided and to the concentration of effort as well as to the attention to standards that it has enforced. It is an old story that specialization has gone so far that except for scholars and scientists with especially capacious minds, academics put their professional standing in some jeopardy as soon as they venture beyond narrow fields. The amateur is vulnerable, and the uses to which the amateur puts knowledge are suspect. An invidious distinction is sometimes drawn, too, between the free-lance "intellectual" and the professional "academic." But what of *amateur* and *intellectual* in the root senses of those words? Are they to be set up in opposition to *professional* when the graduate school seeks to cope with the amplitude of knowledge that the university possesses? Is the knowledge that is not conspicuously pertinent to the professions or not dealt with in professional terms to be thought of, on the model of industrial efficiency, as being no more than the residue of a beneficial but currently unperfected process, something that we should hope and expect continuing professionalization to reduce to nothing? Is it the progress of learning and science in that direction that fires our imaginations? Are we to give every encouragement to the professional approach to knowledge in all its parts and aspects, on the premise that the sum total of professional efforts will constitute the greatest possible advancement of knowledge? Or shall we act upon the idea that the graduate school is neither one more professional school nor the residuary legatee of what is left when explicitly professional schools are created, but rather a trustee of that conception according to which knowledge remains the matrix of human insight, indeed of wisdom, as well as of disciplines and professions yet to be created? That view entails no denigration of professional standards per se, but it does imply that such standards represent the best that has been done, not the most that there still is to do. In the academic fields as in sport, the veteran professionals often show how high the level of technical performance can be pushed, but it remains to be proved that they are the most likely inventors of new games. A graduate school that is professional may be very good indeed and yet not good enough—where advancement of inquiry is the goal.

6. The Meaning of Degrees

In Utopia, degrees and their requirements may not be needed, but in this world, the odds are that the sequel to abolishing the present system would be the emergence of forms with new names but recognizable shapes. We cannot expect to cope with the demands of what amounts to mass education at the graduate level unless some structure that everybody understands can be maintained: the log upon which professor and student sit will itself have to rest upon a complex pedestal. True, the student with intellectual spontaneity has good reason to protest against the piling up of regulations, but many such students will never find themselves in graduate school at all if graduate study is not only organized but also seen to be organized. If the university is not to be a family club, the student not to the academic manner born needs to know that the opportunities for advanced education exist as well as what commitments they entail. It describes but does not itself solve an inherent problem of practicable democracy to say that organization must stop short of bureaucracy. How *is* the apparatus of massive graduate education to be kept from becoming rigidly artificial? The fact that it can become so is sufficiently well documented: the task is to bring degrees and degree requirements, recognized as matters of convention, into the closest possible correspondence with the potentiality of higher study and the need of society that it should flourish.

Again it is easy to make the Ph.D. the butt of criticism and to argue that the requirements of many programs are crippling because the standards of the Ph.D. have been applied where they simply do not fit. Of the Ph.D. octopus, William James warned in 1903: "We ought to look to the future carefully, for it takes generations for a national custom, once rooted, to be grown away from" (James, 1912, p. 342). The present-day critics of the Ph.D. may enjoy the thought of turning the clock backward to the age when winning a Ph.D. was a national custom not yet grown into. What James found repellent, however, was the corruption that occurred when the higher degrees became accepted as the hallmarks of mind, not the institution of higher degrees "for the laudable purpose of stimulating scholarship, especially in the form of 'original research.'" Suppose that the original meaning of the Ph.D. went beyond the terms that James had in mind and that the dynamism of graduate education had its source in a conviction that academic study, in its highest and most open form, should make an original contribution to the intellectual life of the country: the graduate school should advance scholarship and science—emphatically yes; however in doing so it would carry the ideals of American culture and society toward fulfillment. Some academics might be satisified when graduate education succeeded in preparing gifted young people for professional careers in scholarship and science, and plainly graduate education did; but for other academics, that was but a corollary of the idea. Its premise was that inquiry transcended not only a mastery of known facts and laws but also those differences between processes of thought that worked to keep inquiring minds apart: hence the importance attached to the Ph.D. as the emblem of a single quality of mind (ibid., p. 334).

That reading of the past suggests that in the history of graduate education the Ph.D. has been less the villain of the piece than a victim. Which is the more significant today, that the founders of graduate education enabled the Ph.D. to achieve a kind of glory, or that the importance of the degree, in its intended meaning, was obscured when a false emphasis upon degrees as hallmarks of mind (or worse, of personal merit) worked to make having a Ph.D. an end in itself? It would be an academic revolution to restore the Ph.D. to its original meaning, whether in the spirit of Roundhead purification or of a neoclassical attempt to go back to a Golden Age. But the historical case need not be pushed that far. It does indicate what damage can be done when it is forgotten that any degree, as a convention, should stand for something other than itself. The best hope that the graduate school has to determine its own character will be lost if it fails to choose explicitly what the something that each degree represents should be.

Admittedly, the graduate school is not entirely free to enforce its own choice. Sixty years ago, Dean Woodbridge felt obliged to concede that in the American situation traditional ideals of scholarship as the meaning of the Ph.D. had given way to competency to perform certain services. Woodbridge could have made his point by saying that the ideal of the Great American University had proved to be unrealistic. But should the graduate school still be willing to settle for an understanding that graduate degrees show that the holders are competent in particular respects? If so, in which? The quick answer that some academics would give is that graduate degrees, or at least the highest degree, should indicate that the holder is capable of doing research. But what kind of research? When William James was distinguishing between the right and wrong meanings of the higher degrees, he spoke not of research but rather of original research. James used quotation marks, for when he was writing, originality had long since been established as a desirable or even necessary element of research at the level of graduate study. The adjective *original* was less a qualifier of *research* than an epithet—it is difficult to imagine the ceremony where diplomas are conferred explicitly for unoriginal research. If it is true, however, that much work for which degrees are awarded is actually of just that kind, is it the better part of realism to surrender the idea that graduate degrees should stand for originality? There is the distinction, however, between competence in technique and a capacity for original thought and also under the latter rubric, the distinction, or more precisely the gradient, between the study that throws a little more light on an old topic and the discovery that poses a large new question. Should discrete kinds of degrees be instituted to mark the differences between minds that the distinctions suggest? The corollary question is whether the system of degrees should reward competence and originality of thought in empirical research alone or in other modes of inquiry as well—most notably those that illuminate human culture in the large.

The questions involving degrees are many. Should graduate study be thought of as education or as training? Should students be required principally to perform exercises or to attack as yet unsolved problems? Should graduate school be thought of as being professional or not? It is convenient to summarize the debate over graduate education by reference to such pairs of terms, but each set actually defines a range of possible positions or points of emphasis. A graduate school might devote its attention to only a single activity, but most may select a span of activities—e.g., from the range between the studies that are designed entirely to produce technical competence and those where original thought is of the essence. What is necessary is that a rational choice be made and that the system of degrees and degree requirements reflect it accurately. Need it be labored that, in accord with Ockham's razor, a multiplicity of degrees—as measures of what students have achieved—is no less bemusing than none at all might be? It is simplest to begin with the presumption that one degree may be enough and to leave it to practical judgment whether the studies for which a graduate school takes responsibility are so widely separated along the continuum of possibilities that the differences between studies should be formally recognized in the degree system, lest confusion over the meanings of degrees arise.

The permutations of substance and form that are possible in graduate education constitute a great web of choices. Suffice it to cut into the middle by bringing together the propositions already suggested in this essay:

1 *Graduate education is essentially a vehicle of inquiry, which leads the mind out, and as such, graduate education is to be thought of primarily as being indeed education rather than training.* Where other institutions have not been especially designed and established to prepare students to apply existing knowledge, like specific remedies in medicine, in situations that demand attention but raise no questions, it may be necessary for the graduate school of the arts and sciences to fill the gap, but such service to society is not the *raison d'être* of that school. It follows that the starting point for plotting out a degree system is the idea of the generic degree as the outward sign of advanced education toward inquiry, i.e., of a degree telling the public that the recipient has completed a program of education that stresses questioning and the higher processes of thought appropriate to finding answers. It follows, too, that every graduate degree is an "inquiry" degree in the sense that it represents an education informed by the purposes that programs of that kind serve. It does not follow from the proposition that, as a means to an end, training in precisely those same processes can be omitted from graduate education. On the contrary, any degree in the control of the graduate school should imply as a corollary that, in the judgment of the school, the recipient is well trained to engage in some kind of inquiry. The central thrust of the proposition is not that training should not be recognized but rather that a distinction must be drawn between the degrees that represent

technical preparedness for inquiry and those that declare that the recipient has fulfilled the purpose of the school by employing techniques to make a contribution that has actually advanced inquiry. It is rational to grant both kinds of degrees, provided the distinction is observed; and it is honest to grant but a single degree, standing for technical preparedness, and to leave it to the transcript or a letter of appraisal to show that a particular student has exceeded the requirements; but it is neither rational nor honest to grant but a single degree, standing for achievement in the advancement of inquiry, unless the graduate school is ready to flunk candidates of whom no more can be said at the end than that they are well trained.

2 *As a governing force in graduate education, the possibilities of inquiry at any given moment should have a higher claim than existing professional demands.* It is one thing for the graduate school not to be coy about the professional utility of its instruction, to do honor to professional standards, and to educate students who will meet a social need for professional services, but it is another thing for the graduate school to define its relation to inquiry in those terms. That does not mean that a particular degree (e.g., the present M.A.T.) cannot legitimately reflect the fact that the university expects the recipients of the degree to apply their education in a profession to which they may have long since felt themselves called and for which they wish to prepare. What the proposition excludes is neither professional intentions in the mind of the candidate nor a professional ingredient—including the internship—in particular programs but rather any presumption that graduate degrees in a professional aspect, whether by denotation or connotation, should be thought of as summing up what the graduate school of arts and sciences as a whole is about. Where the demand of society is for highly educated professionals, the question is not whether such a school should be professional or educational—which is the falsest kind of dichotomy and an implied libel on the professional schools so designated. Nor is the question whether professionally oriented programs in the graduate school should be relegated to second place in esteem. The question is what idea of education should determine the priorities by which the work of each and every student in the school is governed. Every degree should represent the idea. The proposition is that the graduate school should aim primarily at providing an education toward inquiry as such.

3 *The graduate school should foster the advancement of inquiry both intensively and extensively.* Insistence upon the maintenance of high standards has served, and certainly must continue to encourage, the intensive cultivation of particular methodologies, but it cannot be expected to ensure the full exploration of the processes of thought outside the limits of existing disciplines or of established interdisciplinary groups. Experimentation with new modes of inquiry may in fact be impeded by anxiety over standards, so that regard for them must be balanced by a positive determination to experiment. But should a separate degree be granted for studies oriented toward each of the differing modes of inquiry, e.g., a doctorate for studies stressing empirical research, as now the Ph.D. is often but not exclusively awarded? It would be a disaster if a distinction between degrees gave added encouragement to the candidate for a research degree to ignore the larger context of a particular topic under investigation or allowed the explorer of a wide field to ignore how the facts that support generalization within it were derived and tested empirically. It is not to be supposed, however, that the requirement of overlapping studies need be any less effective in the future than it is now. Emphasis upon hyphenated studies may work increasingly to counteract the inhibiting kind of specialization. The proposition opens up the prospect of a number of counterparts to the "research" degree. The doctor of arts has already appeared, but need it be identified as the "teaching" degree? If new degrees are instituted, they may be known either by the professional use to which the education they represent is put or by the mode of inquiry to which the candidates for each of the degrees are expected principally to direct their minds: hence the possibility of the D.A. as the "synthesis" degree. That identification would correspond to much of the thinking demanded of the instructor in the college classroom but would shift the emphasis of nomenclature toward the kind of intellectual endeavor for which the degree may appropriately be awarded. But does the utility of tags compensate for their unsightliness? The alternative to granting separate degrees is to institute, at one or more levels of accomplishment, a degree that stands generically for inquiry, leaving the specification of particular approaches again to the transcript or letter of appraisal—which is to enlarge upon the original idea of the single doctorate. That principle has the great advantage, if one believes it is such, of emphasizing the unity of inquiry and also of destroying invidious distinctions at the root.

4 *Programs of study should be defined primarily by arriving at the closest match possible between the intellectual bent of the individual student and the whereabouts of the knowledge to which clusters of professors are drawn by their questioning.* That does not mean the abolition of the traditional disciplines as centers of intellectual attraction and as custodians of standards. A very large number of students may always identify their intellectual interests with existing provinces of scholarship and science, and more power to them in their inquiry; however, the allegiance of the student should be determined by intellectual opportunities rather than by institutional requirements. The student whose education cannot be conducted best within the terms appropriate to a department should be free to seek out an ad hoc committee of qualified advisors and to be examined by them, provided, of course, that they have their own freedom to reject ill-considered proposals. But should separate degrees be awarded for such study? There appears to be no particular reason for multiplying degrees to represent nondepartmental studies where standards are high; where they are low, whether in departments or not, there is no good reason for awarding a degree. The proposition gains its force, not from the fact that knowledge is somewhat balkanized, but from the principle of its ecumenical nature. The university will be the better off when the day of identity papers is past.

5 *Graduate study should carry the student with the least avoidable delay to attack the questions that are most worth answering.* It is entirely possible that the student will need some calisthenics in the difficult techniques that alone make much inquiry fruitful; however, the presumption must be that performing exercises, including work on a doctoral dissertation that is defined as an exercise, has no intrinsic merit and should stop at the moment when the student is ready for genuinely original thought—the sooner the better. There is always the risk of the student's moving forward too fast, but where the pros and cons in regard to the student's readiness are in balance, there is the other risk that playing it safe will really mean keeping an adult away from adult thinking longer than is necessary. The stake is not acceleration of careers. True, the shortening up of many dissertation topics cannot be faulted. Sheer, grinding labor—graduate work in the worst sense of the noun—should take as little time as possible, but saving it is not the prime object. Intervals of seemingly wasted time may well be necessary to allow ideas to lie fallow. What matters is the quality of graduate education. Its level is determined not only by the critical mass of qualified professors, of which the Johns Hopkins needed only half a dozen altogether, but also by what may be called a reverberation effect among the students. Its intensity depends upon the number who are highly motivated to devote themselves to inquiry; and inquiry being what it is, no motive is stronger than opportunity to be involved in serious questioning itself. There can be too many human beings in a graduate school for practical comfort, but it is difficult to imagine that there can be too many chances for students to encounter peers—not to speak of professors—who are really thinking. The danger is rather that the centrifugal forces of specialization will prevent students from meeting intellectually often enough. Where the optimum pace of the individual student sets the tempo of academic life, there is little reason to phrase degree requirements in terms either of periods of residence or of courses defined according to segments of the academic year. Fortunately, some graduate schools began long ago to move away from that idea, but a problem of scale does remain. Today the humanist may begin what is prescribed as independent and perhaps original inquiry after only two years of graduate study and spend several years in the library before receiving a degree, while the scientist may well (and for good reasons) spend three or four years as an apprentice member of a scientific team and take a degree before undertaking an inquiry that can be so described. Under the present dispensation, the two students may take doctorates at about the same interval following college graduation, with the humanist perhaps lagging, but the levels of their readiness to move on their own momentum are out of phase, and their degrees, once granted, do not mean quite the same thing. Which is the better part of practical judgment, to continue the present practice, which allows that discrepancy between meanings, or to grasp the nettle and declare that the degree shall be awarded to humanist and scientist alike when independent inquiry begins, or alternatively when the first stage of it ends, but not at different levels of readiness? Such a declaration could create a marked discrepancy between the amounts of time different students spend in the graduate school for the one degree. Should, then, degrees stand for levels of study attained by the individual student?

These propositions yield no single table of degrees; however, they do suggest two patterns. According to the pattern that is closer to current practice, the master's degree would represent completion of a program of studies that carries the education of the student a set distance beyond the college curriculum but still not to full competence in a mode of inquiry or field of knowledge. A version of the degree, e.g., the M.A.T., might be adjusted to explicitly professional requirements. A doctorate would stand for full competence. Each candidate should be sufficiently familiar with cognate modes as not to be inhibited by methodological ignorance and should be sufficiently cultivated to know where the field lies in the intellectual landscape. Each candidate should also complete a study, whether a learned paper, monograph, interpretative essay, critical review of the literature, object of art, etc. —as the chosen mode indicates—to demonstrate ability to use its tools rightly. If only one doctorate is instituted, a letter of appraisal should specify what the bent of the individual candidate is. Award of the degree itself would represent undifferentiated recognition of competence, but the institution of several degrees would of course introduce distinctions. By permitting the recipient of a degree to be identified as a doctor, the university would be identifying itself in turn with the quality of the degree-holder's mind as a fully sharpened instrument. The university should require that the techniques employed by the candidate be brought to bear upon the solution of a problem that the candidate and the supervisors all understand to have significance for the arts and the sciences and perhaps ultimately for intellectual life; however, the university should not declare by the terms of the degree—and such a declaration would but frustrate the person of modest originality—that the candidate's study is designed to be a signally novel contribution to thought. But suppose a particular candidate does actually produce such a contribution: the university then has the option of formally recognizing the fact by awarding the degree with honors. The option is real. It is anomalous to grant honors at the undergraduate but not at the graduate level of studies, but more importantly, it is difficult to correct any public impression that graduate work is humdrum and mechanical if the university does not identify what it thinks work of very high quality is. Nevertheless, would an honors doctorate come simply to constitute another hurdle in an obstacle race toward academic preferment? The risk that it would is great. It may be wiser for the university to take the position— and to do everything in its power to convince the public—that the highest degree does not represent the highest quality of graduate study: do not judge us by degrees alone.

The other pattern is based on the premise that a master's degree should indeed stand for mastery, in which case the degree requirements would be markedly stiffer than they now usually are. A master's thesis would be a masterpiece in the original sense of the word, and the degree itself would represent the same full competence in a mode of inquiry and a field of knowledge as a doctorate would under the terms of the first pattern—and as the Ph.D. does. A degree awarded for mastery, pure and simple, should not be offered in several versions, except to indicate a professional orientation achieved by adding something to the requirements for the nonprofessional degree. Professional preparation that stopped short of full competence in a mode of inquiry and a field of knowledge would be marked by a degree other than the master's, i.e., a degree standing for the holder's readiness to bring education toward inquiry to the fulfillment of professional demands that require competence of their own kind. While the master's would truly stand for mastery, however, it should not be put forward as a testimonial to markedly original accomplishment. The practical advantage of elevating the master's is indeed that as a mark of competence it would not be encumbered, as the Ph.D. is, by other associations that confound the possession of competence and a pledge of brilliance. But again, suppose the candidate demonstrates not only competence with the tools of thought but a capacity for unusually original thinking: there is the option of granting the master's degree with honors or possibly of awarding the doctorate concurrently. But would the doctorate serve any real purpose? The thought is startling, but there remains the possibility of removing the Ph.D. from the system by which careers are advanced and reserving it for inquirers at whatever stage in life who demonstrate by a particular work that they possess in the highest degree the power to teach mankind philosophy—using all three words in their most comprehensive sense. That would indicate to the public what academic study at the highest level is.

But if history teaches any lesson, it is that models are useless if they are presented as mere exercises in futuristic design. They must be viewed in context. It has already been intimated that any innovation may be expected to fail if adjustments could not be made simultaneously in American society and culture. They provide the setting in which the graduate school exists, as if in an electrical field with positive and negative charges. The importance of the social context needs no more illustration than the fact that the issue of professionalism in education takes its point not only from standards sharpened by educational institutions but also from the pressure of accreditation and certification, which have been incorporated into American society at large. It is the wealth of that society that has made an approach to mass education, even at the graduate level, materially possible; it is a democratic ideal of that society that makes the approach an obligation; and it is also the rigidity of some conventions within American society that can frustrate needed change in education. In its cultural aspect, the context is similarly mixed. The university has become more and more influential as the impact of its values, as well as of its expertise, has increased, but the culture authenticates the contribution of the academy differentially. What the professor deems good may or may not be accepted, and what is accepted may or may not be exactly what he intends. Academics today can no more transform graduate education just by proposing models than their predecessors could build universities originally by the same method. But is it necessary — indeed credible — to premise action on the proposition that education is significant only as a creature of the society and culture, and not sometimes as a creator? What began as model building more than a century ago did eventually work such a change that it is impossible to entertain the idea of American life without thinking of the university. It is much of the problem as well as the irony of academic innovation that the obstacles confronting it exist partly because American society, American culture, and the American university are not separable but mutually explanatory terms. If graduate education is to be freed from the burden of convention, the public attitude toward prizes for academic achievement and penalties for academic failure or deprivation must shift drastically. Degrees as a form of social currency are in need of deflation. Even more importantly, the pricing of intellectual ability in that currency at all must be restricted to the markets where such calculations reflect the real needs of the buyer and the particular capacity which the seller supplies: we will know that the transformation to a less artificial and more just ordering of education has been accomplished when the commercial metaphor ceases to be so insistent. Until then, it is neither fruitful to criticize some students for becoming grinds nor intelligent to wonder why other students rebel. But the point need not be labored: what must be remembered is that reform itself will abort if it must always accommodate itself to false expectations.

Can there be any doubt that the wisest course for the university is to work concurrently toward remodeling its own arrangements and toward altering public opinion? It is obvious in which effort the university has the greater initiative and leverage: the presumption must be that the meaning that graduate education has for the public will change only as study within the university itself acquires new meaning. What it is in the future will be heavily influenced by the choices made now between the possible goals, policies, and devices of graduate education. The university patently faces manifold options concerning specific actions that must be supposed to entail critically important effects. But there is another kind of option. It is bound to happen that the university will presently find itself in situations the specifics of which are so far beyond the reach of imagination today that it is fatuous to talk about making decisions in light of them now. In that aspect, the future could simply be left to take care of itself; however, by paying heed to the development of its own culture, the university can hope to influence the quality of mind that is brought to policy making years hence. If self-knowledge is the heart of education, the university can seek to educate itself. As the materials of study are accumulating and a new phase of academic life is already underway, the question is indeed whether the university will fully exploit inquiry into its own nature. Specifically, standards must be subjected to a systematic and continuing audit, which will provide both protection against attack from without and salvation from idiosyncrasy, stuffiness, and decay within. What matters primarily is not that offices of institutional research be set up, that committees be appointed to write self-study reports, or that some professors turn to the examination of academic life as their specialized field, although each of these is a step forward. The stake is deeply informed understanding *of* the university, *across* the university, and not least among graduate students. Those enrolled today will not retire from active life, many of them as academics, until the year 2000 is a memory. What we all think of the university, past and present, is the beginning of the future.

References

Adams, Herbert B.: *The Study of History in American Colleges and Universities,* Bureau of Education, Circular of Information, no. 2, 1887.

Association of American Universities: *Journal of Proceedings and Addresses,* 1900–.

Baker, James H.: statement in *Journal of Proceedings and Addresses of the National Education Association,* pp. 468–471, 1901.

Barnard, John: *From Evangelicalism to Progressivism at Oberlin College, 1866–1917,* Ohio University Press, Athens, 1969.

Becker, Carl: *Cornell University: Founders and the Founding,* Cornell University Press, Ithaca, N.Y., 1943.

Berelson, Bernard: *Graduate Education in the United States,* McGraw-Hill Book Company, New York, 1960.

Bragdon, Henry W.: *Woodrow Wilson, the Academic Years,* Harvard University Press, Cambridge, Mass., 1967.

Burgess, John W.: *Reminiscences of an American Scholar: The Beginnings of Columbia University,* AMS Press, New York, 1966.

Church, Robert L.: "Introduction," in Paul Buck (ed.), *Social Sciences at Harvard, 1860–1920,* Harvard University Press, Cambridge, Mass., 1965.

Council of Graduate Schools in the United States [CGS]: *Proceedings of the Tenth Annual Meeting, "Reassessment,"* December 2–4, 1970.

Donnelly, Walter A. et al.,: *The University of Michigan: An Encyclopedic Survey,* The University of Michigan Press, Ann Arbor, 1953.

Dorfman, Joseph: *Thorstein Veblen and His America,* Augustus M. Kelley Reprints of Economic Classics, New York, 1961.

Dupree, A. Hunter: *Science in the Federal Government: A History of Policies and Activities to 1940,* Harper & Row Publishers, Incorporated, New York, 1964.

Eliot, Charles W.: "The New Education: Its Organization," *Atlantic Monthly,* vol. 23, 1869, pp. 203–220.

"The Embattled University," *Daedalus,* Winter, 1970.

Abrams, Morris B.: "Reflections on the University in the New Revolution," pp. 122–140.

Caws, Peter J.: "Design for a University," pp. 84–107.

Conway, Jill: "Styles of Academic Culture," pp. 43–55.

Dungan, Ralph A.: "Higher Education: The Effort to Adjust," pp. 141–153.

Friedenberg, Edgar Z.: "The University Community in an Open Society," pp. 56–74.

Hoffman, Stanley: "Participation in Perspective?" pp. 177–221.

Kerr, Clark: "Governance and Functions," pp. 108–121.

Luria, S. E., and Zella Luria: "The Role of the University: Ivory Tower, Service Station, or Frontier Post?" pp. 75–83.

Trow, Martin: "Reflections on the Transition from Mass to Universal Higher Education," pp. 1–42.

Fleming, Donald, and Bernard Bailyn (eds.): *The Intellectual Migration: Europe and America, 1930–1960,* Harvard University Press, Cambridge, Mass., 1969.

Furniss, Edgar S.: *The Graduate School of Yale: A Brief History,* New Haven, Conn., 1965.

Hanawalt, Leslie L.: *A Place of Light: The History of Wayne State University,* Wayne State University Press, Detroit, 1968.

Harding, Thomas S.: *College Literary Societies: Their Contribution to Higher Education in the United States, 1815–1876,* Pageant Press International Corp., New York, 1971.

Hawkins, Hugh: *Pioneer: A History of the Johns Hopkins University, 1874–1889,* Cornell University Press, Ithaca, N.Y., 1960.

Hill, Thomas: "Inaugural Address," *Addresses at the Inauguration of Thomas Hill, D.D., as President of Harvard College,* Cambridge, Mass., 1863.

Holt, W. Stull (ed.): *Historical Scholarship in the United States, 1876–1901: As Revealed in the Correspondence of Herbert B. Adams,* The Johns Hopkins University Press, Baltimore, 1938. (The Johns Hopkins University Studies in Historical and Political Science, series 56, no. 4.)

James, William: "The Ph.D. Octopus," in William James, *Memories and Studies,* Longmans, Green & Co., Ltd., London, 1912.

Jencks, Christopher, and David Riesman: *The Academic Revolution,* Doubleday & Company, Inc., Anchor Books, Garden City, N.Y., 1969.

Lilge, Frederic: *The Abuse of Learning: The Failure of the German University,* The Macmillan Company, New York, 1948.

Link, Arthur S.: *Wilson: The Road to the White House,* Princeton University Press, Princeton, N.J., 1947.

Lurie, Edward: *Louis Agassiz: A Life in Science,* University of Chicago Press, 1960.

Madsen, David: *The National University: Enduring Dream of the U.S.A.,* Wayne State University Press, Detroit, 1966.

Maitland, Frederic W.: *Domesday Book and Beyond: Three Essays in the Early History of England,* University Press, Cambridge, England, 1921.

Malone, Dumas: *Jefferson, the Virginian,* Little, Brown and Company, Boston, 1948.

McGrath, Earl J.: *The Graduate School and the Decline of Liberal Education,* Teachers College, Columbia University, New York, 1959.

Morgan, Edmund S.: *The Gentle Puritan, A Life of Ezra Stiles, 1727–1795,* Yale University Press, New Haven, Conn., 1962.

Morison, Samuel E.: *The Founding of Harvard College,* Harvard University Press, Cambridge, Mass., 1935.

Perkins, Dexter, and John Snell: *The Education of Historians in the United States,* McGraw-Hill Book Company, New York, 1962.

Peterson, George E.: *The New England College in the Age of the University,* Amherst College Press, Amherst, Mass., 1964.

Pierson, G. W.: "American Universities in the Nineteenth Century: The Formative Period," in Margaret Clapp (ed.), *The Modern University,* Cornell University Press, Ithaca, N.Y., 1950.

Reed, Glenn A.: "Criticisms of the American Graduate School, 1900–1945," Ph.D. dissertation, Stanford University, September 1950.

Rudolph, Frederick: *The American College and University: A History,* Alfred A. Knopf, Inc. New York, 1962.

Schmidt, George P.: *The Old Time College President,* Columbia University Press, New York, 1930. (Columbia University Studies in History, Economics, and Public Law, no. 317.)

Smith, Wilson: *Professors & Public Ethics: Studies of Northern Moral Philosophers before the Civil War,* Cornell University Press, Ithaca, N.Y., 1956.

Stadtman, Verne A.: *The University of California, 1868–1968,* McGraw-Hill Book Company, New York, 1970.

Storr, Richard J.: *The Beginnings of Graduate Education in America,* The University of Chicago Press, Chicago, 1953.

Storr, Richard J.: *The Environment of Learning: Harper and Chicago,* mimeographed paper prepared for Committee on the Role of Education in American History, Symposium on the Role of Education in Nineteenth-century America, Chatham, Mass., June, 1964.

Storr, Richard J.: *Harper's University: The Beginnings,* University of Chicago Press, Chicago, 1966.

Storr, Richard J.: "Notes on the History of the Social Sciences at Chicago," in *A Report on the Behavioral Sciences at the University of Chicago, October 1, 1954,* University of Chicago, Chicago, 1954, pp. 158–180.

Strothmann, F. W. (for the Committee of Fifteen): *The Graduate School Today and Tomorrow: Reflections for the Profession's Consideration,* Fund for the Advancement of Education, New York, December 1955.

Tewksbury, Donald G.: *The Founding of American Colleges and Universities before the Civil War,* Teachers College, Columbia University, New York, 1932.

Thomas, Russell: *The Search for a Common Learning: General Education, 1800–1960,* McGraw-Hill Book Company, New York, 1962.

Thompson, Daniel G. Brinton: *Ruggles of New York: A Life of Samuel B. Ruggles,* Columbia University Press, New York, 1946.

Tyack, David B.: *George Ticknor and the Boston Brahmins,* Harvard University Press, Cambridge, Mass., 1967.

U.S. Office of Education (USOE): *(a) Enrollment for Master's and Higher Degrees, Fall, 1964: Final Report,* Washington, 1966. *(b) Projection of Educational Statistics to 1975–1976,* Washington, 1966.

Veblen, Thorstein: *The Higher Learning in America: A Memorandum on the Conduct of Universities by Business Men,* B. W. Huebsch, New York, 1918.

Veysey, Laurence R.: *The Emergence of the American University,* University of Chicago Press, 1965.

Wertenbaker, Thomas J.: *Princeton, 1746–1896,* Princeton University Press, Princeton, N.J., 1946.

Wilson, Woodrow: *Congressional Government: A Study in American Politics,* Meridian Books, New York, 1956.

Wolfle, Dael, and Charles V. Kidd: "The Future Market for Ph.D.'s," *Science,* vol. 173, pp. 784–793, August 27, 1971.

Index

This book was set in Vladimir by University Graphics, Inc.
It was printed on acid-free, long-life paper and bound by The
Maple Press Company. The designers were Elliot Epstein and
Edward Butler. The editors were Nancy Tressel, Cheryl Allen,
and Janine Parson for McGraw-Hill Book Company and Verne A.
Stadtman and Sidney J. P. Hollister for the Carnegie Commission
on Higher Education. Joe Campanella supervised the production.

DATE DUE

GAYLORD			PRINTED IN U.S.A